A Traveler's
GUIDE
to the
AFTERLIFE

"People interested in the research of survival of physical death will find in *A Traveler's Guide to the Afterlife* a compelling wealth of information. People who are not interested in the subject will benefit from the author's erudition and his remarkable exploration of the sacred Eastern and Western traditions."

ANABELA CARDOSO, RETIRED PORTUGUESE SENIOR CAREER DIPLOMAT, EDITOR IN CHIEF OF THE *ITC JOURNAL,* AND AUTHOR OF *ELECTRONIC VOICES: CONTACT WITH ANOTHER DIMENSION?*

"An extraordinary exploration of humankind's collective wisdom about what lies on the other side of death."

MATTHEW MCKAY, PH.D., AUTHOR OF *SEEKING JORDAN*

"What stands out in this traveler's guide to the afterlife is how great minds throughout Earth's history have over and over said that reincarnation, the recycling of souls, is the machinery of the universe. This book reinforces the importance of the soul in the mind-body-spirit complex that humans are; it should inspire all readers to do what they can to strengthen their soul while alive in the matter world."

LINDA MOULTON HOWE, EMMY AWARD–WINNING INVESTIGATIVE JOURNALIST AND REPORTER AND EDITOR OF EARTHFILES.COM

"I have been hoping to find a resource like this for years. Mark's book has become one of my most valuable reference tools for information on multicultural, multispiritual perspectives on death and the afterlife. The research is impeccable."

Rev. Terri Daniel, CT, founder of
the Death Awareness Institute and
The Afterlife Conference

"The suspense of death often kills us, figuratively speaking. That unknown door we all inevitably walk through stands as the proverbial 'elephant in the room' that we all choose to ignore. In this book Mark Mirabello has accumulated the most extensive knowledge on death and the afterlife; it is enough to make a believer out of the skeptic. After reading this book you will face that unknown door with no suspense but instead a sense of wonder and excitement."

Jason Gregory, author of
Enlightenment Now and
The Science and Practice of Humility

A Traveler's GUIDE *to the* AFTERLIFE

Traditions and Beliefs on
Death, Dying, and What Lies Beyond

Mark Mirabello, Ph.D.

Inner Traditions
Rochester, Vermont • Toronto, Canada

Inner Traditions
One Park Street
Rochester, Vermont 05767
www.InnerTraditions.com

Library of Congress Cataloging-in-Publication Data

Names: Mirabello, M. L. (Mark Linden), author.
Title: A traveler's guide to the afterlife : traditions and beliefs on death, dying, and
  what lies beyond / Mark Mirabello.
Description: Rochester, Vermont : Inner Traditions, 2016. | Includes
  bibliographical references and index.
Identifiers: LCCN 2016007919 (print) | LCCN 2016008357 (e-book) |
  ISBN 9781620555972 (paperback) | ISBN 9781620555989 (e-book)
Subjects: LCSH: Future life. | BISAC: BODY, MIND & SPIRIT / Reincarnation.
  | RELIGION / Mysticism. | SOCIAL SCIENCE / Death & Dying.
Classification: LCC BL535 .M53 2016 (print) | LCC BL535 (e-book) |
  DDC 202/.3—dc23
LC record available at http://lccn.loc.gov/2016007919

Printed and bound in the United States

10 9 8 7 6 5 4 3 2

Text design by Priscilla Baker and layout by Virginia Scott Bowman
This book was typeset in Garamond Premier Pro with Caslon and Gill Sans used
as display typefaces

To send correspondence to the author of this book, mail a first-class letter to the
author c/o Inner Traditions • Bear & Company, One Park Street, Rochester, VT
05767, and we will forward the communication, or contact the author directly at
www.markmirabello.com.

*In an underground Mithraic temple, in Sarrebourg, France,
archaeologists discovered a human skeleton, chained to the altar.
The door was found blocked, so the nameless follower of Mithras
had died alone and in darkness.*

＊ ⸱ ＊

*To the unknown individual who was murdered
for his religion, I dedicate this book.*

If you know what you sing, death is the center of a long life.

LUCAN

The only true wisdom lives far from mankind, out in the great loneliness, and it can be reached only through suffering. Privation and suffering alone can open the mind of a man to all that is hidden in others.

IGJUGARJUK (INUIT SHAMAN)

I have always imagined that Paradise will be a kind of library.

JORGE LUIS BORGES

Whatever is here is found elsewhere. But whatever is not here is nowhere else.

MAHABHARATA

Contents

Acknowledgments

I wish to thank several colleagues, including professors Lavanya Vemsani, Sean Dunn, Sibylle Herrmann, and James Miller at Shawnee State University, as well as the late John L. Kelley, professor emeritus. I also wish to thank Jack Wolf, Kwak Ho-Sung, Tricia Martineau Wagner, Carol Sue Sessor, Erica Hasselbach, Zachary Nickoli, Mogg Morgan, Heather Cantrell, Jon Graham, Nancy Yeilding, Jamaica Burns Griffin, Blythe Bates, and a future professor named Ashley Rowland.

I wish also to remember family members, especially Paula Sheroian, Paul Mirabello, Regina Baranski Mirabello, Jennifer Greca, Stacey Treanor, Brad Sheroian, Ashley Oliker, Donald Sheroian, Frank Vallas, Margaret Vallas, Mae Mirabello, Martha and Jack Lickendorff, Amy Gilmore, Grace Russo Mirabello, Leonardo Mirabello, Nadine Maynard, Viola Shope, and Lailah Holbrook.

Finally, I wish to thank my wife, Taryn Mirabello, who has always inspired me. She is a loving soul enveloped in beauty and light.

Note from the Editor

The author has drawn on 965 sources in the creation of this book, texts from around the globe and throughout time. While not every source is quoted directly, each of these texts has informed the book.

Given the large number of sources, a condensed endnote/bibliography style has been used. Each source is listed alphabetically in a numbered list at the end of the book. In the body of the text, a superscript number refers readers to these sources.

A large portion of these source texts have been published multiple times, by different publishers and in different periods of time—and, indeed, the author often consulted more than one edition of a given text. Because of this, the author has provided only author names and book titles rather than referencing a specific edition or printing.

For some facts and quotes, multiple sources are given. Simple facts are open to different interpretations, and those readers intrigued by a particular belief or culture may wish to consult various sources for additional information and commentary from different perspectives. When multiple note numbers are provided, the author considers the first source(s) to be the most significant.

Introduction

The sage keeps company with those who think of life and death just as one thinks of waking and sleeping, not with those who have forgotten the meaning of return.

LIEH TZU

Death is often only the result of our indifference to immortality.

MIRCEA ELIADE, *IMAGES AND SYMBOLS*

Where joy and delight reign, where reigns pleasure heaped upon pleasure, where the heart's desires are attained, in this place, make me immortal.

RIG VEDA

Sigmund Freud (1856–1939) made this observation: "It is indeed impossible to imagine our own death; and whenever we attempt to do so we can perceive that we are still present as spectators."[317]

I have tried to imagine myself dead. . . .

Perhaps, like a Brahmin priest, I am shrouded in silk, garlanded with flowers, drenched in clarified butter, and cremated on a pyre of scented wood until my skull explodes from the heat.[442, 175]

1

Or, perhaps, as the Marquis de Sade (1740–1814) requested, I am buried in the forest, the soft earth above me strewn with acorns.[260, 346]

Or, perhaps, like some of the tribal people in India, I am buried face down in a grave filled with thorns.[72]

Or, perhaps, like a Tibetan Buddhist, I am given a "sky burial." My body is taken to a hill-top, chopped into pieces, and left for the birds to consume.[663]

But, as Freud predicted, I cannot *really* imagine myself dead. I am presently stricken with cancer—I am surrounded by skulls and carrion flowers, the symbols of death—but I cannot *really* imagine myself dead.

So, this is not a book about death—about annihilation—to the contrary, it is a book about *existence* beyond death. It is about *surviving* the grisly decay of the grave.

In my opinion, a volume on death, a form of literary necrophilia, is informative but of finite value. A text on the afterworlds, however, is a torch that illuminates the great unknown.

Moreover, information about the afterlife is valued by all responsible minds. As one Buddhist text makes clear, since death is virtually inevitable (even the Buddha died), to simply focus on enjoying life here is as misguided as a person who has fallen off a cliff deciding to enjoy his descent to earth.[535]

With information, however, we can die without fear and without confusion.

SELECTED GUIDANCE

Imagine that this book is a treasure concealed in a lead casket. For special eyes only, the eyes of the adept, this slender volume is a guide—a breviary—for those who will one day cross the threshold of death.

Designed for the living and those yet unborn, it is a "traveler's guide" to other worlds.

Many such books have been written before—the *Book of Going Forth by Day* in venerable Egypt, the *Katha Upanishad* in mysterious India, the *Bardo Thodol* in fabled Tibet, the golden Orphic tablets in classical Greece, and *Heaven and its Wonders and Hell: From Things Heard and Seen* in eighteenth-century Europe—but this work is different. Unlike religious texts, this book has no scriptural pretensions.

As I researched this work, I focused on interesting or unusual concepts about the afterlife, and my aim was *judicious selection* rather than exhaustive coverage. Obviously, since approximately 3,500 known societies have existed on the earth[839]—and many of these have distinctive ideas about the afterworld—some culling was necessary.

For the record, I have tried to avoid the idealistic twaddle of the pseudo-occultists, the boilerplate sermons of the established religions, the unadulterated bilge of self-proclaimed prophets, the ontological nonsense of the hack metaphysicians, and the smug nihilism of the scientific materialists.

I have no salvationist agenda. There are no dogmas here—simply fragments of ideas—gathered from many cultures across time and space.

I share these fragments *without* certainty. Moreover, I share them with a certain amount of humility.

I am mindful of the fact that, according to Lao Tzu (flourished in the fifth or fourth century BCE), the distinguished sage who, according to legend, was born an old man,[585] "Those who speak do not know; those who know do not speak."[261, 671, 508]

A similar notion is found in the Upanishads, the great religious texts from India.[140]

Nevertheless, I have written the book.

A WORD ON SOURCES

Like the terrifying Death's-Head Hawkmoth[368]—with the skull pattern on its thorax and its weird melancholy cry, characteristics that inspired the Edgar Allan Poe story *The Sphinx*—I have raided many hives belonging to many different bees.

In other words, I have tried to examine the complete human experience.

Too many books focus on modern religions—the great faiths—and too many people view the arcane religions and mystery cults either as living relics or as dead anthropological curiosities.

But, the human race has spent most of its existence "grubbing, hunting, killing, feasting, mating, dying, and giving birth,"[293] and "civilization" is a relatively recent innovation.[818] Indeed, as is well known, as recently as 1500 CE, only one-third of the inhabited world was "civilized"—the rest was pre-literate and tribal.

Besides, traditional peoples, such as hunters and nomads—fierce people living under the sky and stalking great quadrupeds—may have glimpsed the truth, so why ignore them?

Moreover, as Diodorus Siculus (flourished 30 BCE) reminds us in his *Library of History,* when truth is corrupted, and knowledge degenerates, remote "barbarian" people may preserve it unspoilt.

Of course, as the learned Professor Mircea Eliade (1907–1986) noted, ideas do not leave tangible fossils,[261] so it is difficult to determine what archaic people actually believed, but an attempt has been made.

A WORD TO THE SKEPTICS

In antiquity, so firm was the Celtic belief in an afterlife, wrote Pomponius Mela (died circa 45 CE), that "some even used to defer paying debts until their arrival in the next world."[739, 387, 247]

But is immortality simply a childish dream?

To the contrary, immortals once dominated the earth. Indeed, for countless eons, there was no natural death on the planet.[854]

Like the pagan gods of Odinism, these primordial immortals could be killed,[592] but they did not "self-destruct in a programmed way" as humans do. They did not grow old and die.[854, 103]

Who were these immortals? Reproducing without sex,[424] they exist to this day, and we call them *bacteria*. Some of them may be millions of years old.[103] And they are incredibly common. In fact, between two and nine pounds of our weight is bacteria, mostly in our intestines.[812, 103]

Fantastically prolific, bacteria like E. coli (*Escherichia coli*) double their numbers every fifteen minutes, and if they all lived, in two days the "daughters of one E-coli would weigh as much as the human race."[103] A few days later, they would outweigh all living things on earth. Soon, they would outweigh our planet.[454, 103]

Fortunately for the human race, however, bacteria colonies do not even grow to the size of a penny. Placed in a dish of nutrients in a lab, they die because they exhaust their food supply and eventually suffocate in their own waste products.[454]

Humans can learn from bacteria.

A WORD ON STYLE

The ancient Egyptians dealt with the "other side" in a matter-of-fact way—their texts never speak of inexplicable doctrines or union with the absolute[405, 41]—and neither do I. I have tried to discuss all ideas in a clear and concrete fashion.

The reader will note that when I describe religious beliefs—including the concepts of apparently dead religions—I use the present tense.

Why?

Great ideas—especially great religious ideas—are timeless. What the legendary Carl Jung (1875–1961) said about mythic archetypes also applies to religious ideas:

> Archetypes are like riverbeds which dry up when the water deserts them, but which it can find again at any time. An archetype is like an old watercourse along which the water of life has flowed for centuries, digging a deep channel for itself. The longer it has flowed in this channel the more likely it is that sooner or later the water will return to its old bed.[453]

The ancient Egyptians of the Old Kingdom period had no past tense in their language,[42] and modern humanity can learn from that.

I

Where Are We Now?

Euripides Said
We May Be Already Dead

You have not awakened to wakefulness, but to a previous
dream. That dream is enclosed within another, and so on
in to infinity. . . . You will die before you ever really awake.
                                                    JORGE LUIS BORGES,
                                                    "THE GOD'S SCRIPT"

Both sleep and waking are misnomers. We are only
dreaming. . . . We dream that we are awake; we dream
that we are asleep.

                                                    NISARGADATTA MAHARAJ

The things of this world can be truly perceived only by
looking at them backwards.
                                        BALTHASAR GRACIAN, *THE CRITIC*

The universe is a machine for the making of Gods.
                                        HENRI BERGSON, *THE TWO SOURCES*
                                                    OF MORALITY AND RELIGION

I did exist in the past, not that I did not; I will exist in the future, not that I will not; and I do exist in the present, not that I do not.

BUDDHA

Science, in one aspect, is ordered technique; in another, it is rationalized mythology.

JOHN DESMOND BERNAL, *SCIENCE IN HISTORY*

For beings whose senses are different from ours the universe is different.

ALAIN DANIÉLOU, *MYTHS AND GODS OF INDIA*

William Shakespeare (1564–1616) eloquently called death "the undiscovere'd country,"[778] but, in reality, we have no idea where we are *now*.

With our five senses and our scientific instruments, we think we know a great deal about the cosmos, but we may be deluded.

As in the Hindu story, we may be like the frog at the bottom of the well. The frog's view is restricted—he sees only the dark water, the slimy walls of the well, and the circle of sky above—and he believes that he is observing the whole universe, as it is.[890]

But, if our experience is limited, and our knowledge is incomplete, what is true?

We think that this universe is *the* universe, but that may not be correct. In Buddhist cosmology, the Mahayana sutras reveal the presence of billions of universes like our own,[535] and according to the "many worlds interpretation" of physicist Hugh Everett III (1930–1982), there are other universes and quite likely other versions of ourselves in them.[865]

Moreover, although the universe appears solid and real to us, in a sense we are phantoms in a phantom world. In the words of Nicholas Maxwell (born 1937), a philosopher of science, "We now know that material objects are in fact primarily energy and empty space; the few particles that really exist, like protons and electrons, never touch each other at all."[71]

In effect, 99.999999999999 percent of an atom's volume appears to be just empty space![864]

If we constructed a scale model of a hydrogen atom, with its proton being the size of a basketball, its one electron would be the size of a pencil dot and would be eleven miles away.[25]

To state the emptiness another way, "the distance between the nucleus and the edge of the atom, from the electron's perspective, is greater than the distance between the earth and the moon from our perspective."[864]

Or, consider this point. We believe that we live in an inorganic universe, but could the entire universe be alive? Not only is this idea found in Hinduism,[481] but the Catholic priest, Salvador Freixedo, suggested that the "earth is like a cell in a giant organism, an organism so large that we can imagine it but not see it."[316]

Regarding size, we assume that we are in a vast universe, but perhaps we, as humans, are simply diminutive beings. According to the *Sefer Razi'el,* a Jewish mystical book ascribed to the angel Raziel, the Jewish god is 2,300,000,000 *parasangs* high, or 7.2 billion miles (Pluto is 4.6 billion miles from the sun). In the *Soundarya Lahari,* a Hindu text, it is said that the entire universe is from a speck of dust on the foot of the goddess called Mahadevi.[481]

Or, regarding size, perhaps our smallness is simply relative. The Raelian movement, which is based on reputed extraterrestrial contact, argues that our galaxy is simply a molecule in a larger universe, and our molecules are the galaxies of smaller universes.[709, 667]

The Raelian idea is found in the *Bhagavata Purana,* a Hindu text, which makes this statement: "There are innumerable universes besides this one, and although they are unlimitedly large, they move about like atoms in you. Therefore you are called unlimited."[81]

Moreover, we believe that we occupy an old universe—Aristotle

(384–322 BCE), as Diodorus Siculus (flourished 30 BCE) pointed out, thought the universe and the human race had always existed[130]—and modern science claims that the cosmos is billions of years old—but it is possible that the cosmos was created three heartbeats ago.

Jorge Luis Borges (1899–1986), the great Argentinian writer, in his classic story, "Tlon, Uqbar, Orbis Tertius," refers to Bertrand Russell's conjecture that our planet was created a few moments ago and was provided with a humanity that remembers an "illusionary past."[747] The idea is also discussed in *Omphalos* by Philip Henry Gosse (1810–1888).[348]

We also assume that the universe has an independent existence, but it may not. According to some Muslim philosophers—advocates of what is called Ash'ari theology—Allah is continually destroying and recreating the universe from moment to moment.[799, 865]

Impossible?

Oddly, modern quantum field theory argues that we are being annihilated and reformed many times per second.[865]

Also, we *assume* that we are in the universe of the living, and the dead, if they exist, are elsewhere, but, in fact, *we* may be dead right now.

Could this universe in fact be the realm of the dead? The ancient Greeks observed that birth here is unpleasant—we leave a warm dark womb and are thrust into a world of terrifying lights and sounds—while death here can be pleasant, even pleasurable. Freshly killed soldiers and recently hanged men have erect genital organs.[362] And, as G. Devereux pointed out, "As any big game hunter knows, at the moment of death a male animal's sexual organ becomes tumescent and emits semen."[131]

Therefore, could we in fact be dead? Could our deaths here actually be births into life? In the words of the ancient Greek writer Euripides (circa 480–406 BCE), "Who knows then whether Life be not Death, and what we here call Death be called Life there below?"[738]

And in *Lieh Tzu,* an ancient Chinese Taoist text attributed to Lie Yukou (flourished circa 400 BCE), these words appear: "Death and life, they are a going and returning: being dead here, how do I know that it is not being alive there?"[261]

Or, consider this possibility: perhaps we do not exist at all. Nick Bostom, an Oxford University professor, suggests that we may be in a computer simulation. A popular film, written by Lana Wachowski (born in 1965) and Andrew Paul Wachowski (born in 1967), describes a dystopia in which unconscious humans are plugged into a computer simulation, but Bostom is not referring to that situation. He suggests we may simply be bits of information in a powerful computer.[256]

Or, consider this possibility: perhaps our universe exists only in the mind. The followers of Yogacara, a philosophical school originating in India, embraced the "mind-only" doctrine, and they describe the world as a property of consciousness. Matter, it is possible, may be "merely certain kinds of ideas in the mind."[70]

Indeed, Sir James Jeans (1877–1946), the celebrated English physicist, astronomer, and mathematician, noted that the universe is "more like a great thought" than "a great machine."[440]

Or, consider this possibility: perhaps our universe, with its luminous suns and mysterious worlds, is merely a dream.

According to the *Yoga Vasistha,* a Hindu book written before the twelfth century of the current era, we cannot wake up from the dream because it is very literally someone else's dream.[890] Thus, according to Professor Wendy Doniger, *enlightenment* means "staying asleep but being aware that you are dreaming."[238, 954]

According to the Hindus, the god Brahma daydreams the universe for one day in *his* time, but this daydream lasts 34 billion, 360 million years in human time. Brahma then experiences a night of equal length, and during that time the universe disappears. The next day, however, he daydreams again.[204]

A related notion, suggested by Charles Fort (1874–1932) in his *Book of the Damned,* is that we are all living in someone else's *novel.* The novel, noted Fort, is not a particularly good one.[494, 309]

Or, to return to the dream idea, perhaps the dream could be our dream. Professor H. H. Price (1899-1984), the Welsh philosopher, made this point: "It is plausible to suggest that we are dreaming all day long as well as at night, but only notice it when we are asleep."[285, 699]

Indeed, Descartes (1596–1650), the philosopher and the inventor of analytic geometry, said that we cannot prove we are not dreaming *now.*[230]

Of course, that dream could be a nightmare. In the words of Geshe Kelsang Gyatso (born 1931), a Buddhist:

> Since beginningless time sentient beings like oneself have been trapped in the nightmare of *samsara* because we have never awoken from the sleep of ignorance, not realizing that all our suffering is just the creation of our own confused mind.[363]

But, how could a dream seem real?

Nagarjuna (circa 150–250 CE), one of the founding "fathers" of Mahayana Buddhism, made this statement:

> In a dream one rejoices although there is nothing enjoyable, one is angry although there is nothing to annoy, one is frightened although there is nothing to frighten. So do the beings with regard to the things of the world.[963, 614]

If this universe is a dream, perhaps the prediction of Chuang-tzu (fourth century BCE), the Taoist sage from China, will come to pass: "Some day there will be a great awakening when we shall know that all this is a dream."[92, 261]

And perhaps, as the *Yoga Vasistha* suggests, "Death is but waking from a dream."[890]

II

How to Live Forever without a God or an Immortal Soul

If Either Eternal Recurrence or Eternalism Is Correct, Scientific Skepticism May Be Groundless

For, 'tis one of their tenets that nothing perisheth, but (as the sun and year) everything goes in a circle, lesser or greater, and it is renewed and refreshed in its revolutions.

ROBERT KIRK,
THE SECRET COMMONWEALTH

I come again and again in all eternity to this identical and selfsame life, so that I may again teach the eternal return of all things.

FRIEDRICH NIETZSCHE,
THUS SPAKE ZARATHUSTRA

It is all one to me where I am to begin; for I shall return there again.

PARMENIDES

Skepticism about the afterlife is actually quite ancient. One philosophical school in India–the Lokayata or "worldly" school—rejects reincarnation. When the body is destroyed, they argue, the spirit, which is created by the body, dissolves into nothingness. They insist that the Vedas, the sacred texts of India, are the worthless prattling of fools, and they believe that physical sense data is the only source of knowledge.[238]

Such ideas, which are more than twenty-five centuries old, are common today.

Indeed, modern scientists, who have a pathological disbelief in spirit, believe that we are simply biological beings in a world without meaning or purpose.[305, 369] In the vastness of time, they say, we exist only briefly: from the discharge of semen to the inhumation or cremation.

The scientists believe that we are only a "meat body." Mostly water with a few added impurities,[915] almost 99 percent of the mass of the human body is composed of six elements: oxygen, carbon, hydrogen, nitrogen, calcium, and phosphorus.[955] About 0.85 percent is composed of only five elements: potassium, sulfur, sodium, chlorine, and magnesium. There are also a few trace elements, such as fluorine.[386]

Somehow, say the scientists, these elements, in the proper mixture, produce life. It is unclear how, but, as physicist Niels Bohr (1885–1962) pointed out, who could deduce the marvelous quality of water's "wetness" simply by observing hydrogen and oxygen?[447]

The Greek philosopher Heraclitus (circa 535–circa 475 BCE) described consciousness as "an enormous space whose boundaries, even by traveling along every path, could never be found out,"[439, 206] and a Tibetan Buddhist adept is trained to move his consciousness to his hand, or, even more remarkably, to a statue, an incense stick, or a tree (the technique is described by Alexandra David-Neel in *Magic and Mystery in Tibet*), but modern scientists claim that the mind is simply located in and produced by the brain.

Indeed, Jakob Moleschott (1822–1893), the Dutch physiologist, famously declared: "The brain secretes thought as the kidney secretes urine."[843]

A nondescript organ, the human brain is 60 percent fat,[468] and it has the consistency of a half-set jell. In most adults, it weighs approximately three pounds, although Dr. John Lorber (1915–1996), a University of Sheffield professor, studied a mathematics student, with an IQ of 126, who had virtually no brain. (The young man's skull was lined with a thin layer of brain cells about one millimeter in thickness. The rest of his skull was filled with "cerebrospinal fluid.")[960, 797, 181, 919]

DEATH AS DECOMPOSITION

When the brain dies, insist the nihilists, the mind dies.[441] The materialists, who are nihilists, claim that there is no soul.

Interestingly, some extreme materialists—some psychologists in the Behaviorism school—argue that since consciousness cannot be subjected to measurement—and cannot be directly observed in the laboratory—there is also no such thing as consciousness![501] There is only brain.

According to the nihilists, death is final. In the words of Bertrand Russell (1872–1970), the British philosopher, "no fire, no heroism, no intensity of thought or feeling, can preserve a life beyond the grave."[454] And that means everyone. As the physicist Frank J. Tipler opined, "I do not think Jesus really rose from the dead. I think he rotted in some grave."[865]

When you die, say the materialists and the nihilists, all that you were simply decomposes. Within three or four days after death, the brain liquefies and can be poured out of a hole in the skull.[701, 151] Ultimately, your entire body rots and only ozone and fertilizer remain.[720] In short, the destiny of man is to be transformed into good, nourishing soil.[519]

Of course, if you fear becoming meat for worms, you can be cremated. In that case, you become five to seven pounds of ash and pulverized bone.[463]

CIRCULAR TIME

But, even if you die and decompose—even if your "soul," as Aristotle (384–322 BCE) believed, dies with you[560]—you may still, in a sense, live forever.

How can such a thing be possible?

Judaic-Christian thought has conditioned us to think of linear time (so-called one-dimensional time)—that there is a unique beginning, a unique history, and a unique end—but, in fact, time might be a circle.[367]

Indeed, as Aristotle suggested, if time has no end, it must be circular. Aristotle said what is eternal is circular and what is circular is eternal.[227]

The idea of circular time, called the "eternal recurrence of the same," has been discussed by philosophers such as Pythagoras (570–495 BCE), David Hume (1711–1776), and Friedrich Nietzsche (1844–1900).[383]

How can time be circular? Matter, as David Hume pointed out, can be arranged only in a finite number of ways. And, given infinite time, repetition MUST occur.

In his *Dialogues Concerning Natural Religion,* Hume (in opaque eighteenth-century prose) makes this observation:

> A finite number of particles is only susceptible of finite transpositions: and it must happen, in an eternal duration, that every possible order or position must be tried an infinite number of times. This world, therefore, with all its events, even the most minute, has before been produced and destroyed, and will again be produced and destroyed, without any bounds and limitations. No one, who has a conception of the powers of infinite, in comparison of finite, will ever scruple this determination.[416]

Likewise, Henri Poincaré (1854–1912), the great scientist, theorized that given enough time, every closed system returns to its initial state.

Given infinite time and infinite space, the eternal return is a mathematical certainty.[367, 151, 684]

Think of a game of chess.

In chess, there are perhaps $10^{100,000}$ possible chess games. To help understand the size of that figure, scholars estimate there are 10^{15} hairs on all human heads, 10^{23} grains of sand on all the earth's beaches, and 10^{81} atoms in the universe.[256]

If two eternal chess masters played forever, however, they must eventually repeat their earlier games *move for move*. This must happen because there are a finite number of possible games of chess.[367]

If eternal recurrence is real—if (as Nietzsche said) history repeats itself on a grand scale, and if (as one pagan religion asserts) "time is an endless circle in which all possible destinies are repeated forever,"[592]—that means that we will live again, but not in any other world.[821]

One of the consequences of eternal recurrence is that each individual is immortal, although not continuously. Each person has an infinite number of bodies (each of these bodies is the same as the body we have now), and each individual has an infinite number of lives (always the same life) distributed throughout eternity.

Between each life, there are immense periods of time—billions, even trillions or quadrillions of years—when the body that you have now does not exist. However, there is no time before which or after which you do not exist. You will always exist again. "You are born, you live, and you die infinitely often."[821]

Eternal return is "a kind of resurrection without any judgment, reward, or punishment."[821] In the circle of time, you return to life in your own body on this earth, and you will experience "the eternal repetition of identical events."[383]

In *Thus Spake Zarathustra,* Nietzsche makes this observation: "The soul is as mortal as the body. But the knot of causes in which I am entwined recurs and will create me again."[627]

In *Gay Science,* Nietzsche uses these words to describe the phenomenon:

This life as you now live it and have lived it, you will have to live once more and innumerable times more; and there will be nothing new in it, but every pain and every joy and every thought and sigh and everything unutterably small and great in your life will have to return to you, and all in the same succession and sequence.[626]

Meaning, as Sir Thomas Browne (1605–1682) noted in his *Religio Medici* in 1643: "And in this sense, I say, the world was before the Creation, and at an end before it had a beginning; and thus was I dead before I was alive."[123]

ETERNALISM

According to "eternal recurrence of the same," we will live again—we will repeat our lives exactly—because time is a circle. We will die an infinite number of times, but we will never die forever.

But, what if time does not pass at all? Does that mean that death is not the end?

Indeed, it does.

According to a philosophic notion called eternalism, described by a Cambridge philosophy professor named J. M. E. McTaggart, who wrote "The Unreality of Time" in 1908, all points in time are equally "real." Eternalism stands in contrast to the "presentist" idea that only the present is real.[578, 367]

The concept of eternalism, also called the "eternal now" in Hinduism, is the state in which "everything is everywhere and always," and "every point of space touches every point of time."[656] In Buddhist philosophy, the idea that the past, present, and future exist is found in the Sarvastivada school of thought.[261] *Sarvasti* means "all exists."[120]

In ancient Greek thought, the idea is implicit in the thought of the great philosopher Parmenides (flourished sixth or fifth century BCE).[54, 675]

If eternalism is correct, right now—somewhere—your great-grandmother is a two-year-old girl playing on the floor. Right now—

somewhere—it is the year 2190. Right now—somewhere—Judas is betraying Jesus. Right now—somewhere—you are a young person enjoying your first kiss.

In other words, "yesterday exists," as the Russian scholar P. D. Ouspensky (1878–1947) says in the *Strange Life of Ivan Osokin,* and so does tomorrow.

In the view suggested by eternalism, there is no passage of time. In effect, the ticking of a clock measures durations between events much as the marks on a measuring tape measure the distances between places.[199, 252]

Julian Barbour, a British physicist, argues in *The End of Time* that we have *no evidence* of the past except for our memory of it, and *no evidence* of the future except for our belief in it. Change, he argues, creates an illusion of time, but in fact each individual moment always exists.[54]

Likewise, Professor Fred Hoyle (1915–2001), the esteemed English astronomer, suggested that the idea of time as an ever-rolling stream is "a grotesque and absurd illusion." Hoyle said that everything that was and will be exists "all the time." Consciousness, said Hoyle, is creating false ideas about the past, the present, and the future.[713, 344, 410]

Perhaps the Hopi Indians, a traditional nation in aboriginal North America, understood reality. In the Hopi language, there are no past or future tenses or concepts.[574]

Of course, if everything does indeed exist all the time, and if eternalism is correct, that means the fear of death is pointless.

As Billy Pilgrim explains in *Slaughterhouse Five,* the novel by Kurt Vonnegut (1922–2007), "When a person dies, he only appears to die. He is still very much alive in the past. . . . All moments, past, present, and future, always have existed, always will exist."[899]

III

Information for the Nihilists

A Guide for the Metaphysically Impaired

As to the soul, and the belief that it is immortal by nature, or may hope to attain to immortality, as I have taught you—all this they will mock at, and will even persuade themselves that it is false. No word of reverence or piety, no utterance worthy of heaven and of the gods of heaven, will be heard or believed.

And so the gods will depart from mankind. . . .

PROPHECY OF HERMES IN THE *DIALOGUE BETWEEN HERMES TRISMEGISTUS AND ASCLEPIUS*

In the last analysis magic, religion, and science are nothing but theories of thought; and as science has supplanted its predecessors, so it may hereafter be itself superceded by some more perfect hypothesis, perhaps by some totally different way of looking at the phenomena—of registering the shadows on the screen—of which we in this generation can form no idea.

SIR JAMES FRAZER, *THE GOLDEN BOUGH*

> *When . . . the hegemony of the Church began to wane, it was replaced by a new religion or pseudoreligion, one that denied the existence of any reality other than the purely physical and mechanical, and which sought to govern life and behavior of humanity solely on the basis of physical laws (or some interpretation of them). The only reality, says the new religion, is quantity; what cannot be weighed or measured or counted does not exist, or might as well not exist.*
>
> RICHARD SMOLEY, FOREWORD TO
> GODWIN'S *THE GOLDEN THREAD*

In the last few centuries, religion in the West has been subjected to what Eliphas Levi (1810–1875) called the "hostility of the learned."[524] Thus, Sigmund Freud (1856–1939), an atheist descended from Jews, called religion an "obsessional neurosis" and a regression to infantile forms of behavior.[716]

And Charles Binet-Sanglé (1868–1941), the author of a four-volume work called *The Madness of Jesus* (*La Folie de Jésus*), argued that Jesus was mentally ill and suffered from "religious paranoia."[653]

Given such prejudices, it is not surprising that learned anthropologists somehow think it is significant that chimpanzees have been seen to dance in the presence of waterfalls and thunderstorms.[671] The suggestion here is that religion—and ritual—are so primitive that even brute beasts engage in such behavior.

It is also not surprising that the West, as the late Professor Heinrich Zimmer (1890–1943) pointed out, has had no new metaphysics since the middle of the eighteenth century![962]

UNDOING ASSUMPTIONS

Given such prejudices, it is necessary to first remove some rather puerile "Western" assumptions about the afterlife. Most Westerners assume that *if* there is an afterlife, then we must have one immortal soul, that our status in the otherworld must be determined by faith or morals or both, and that heaven and hell must be forever.

The traditional Christian heaven was described by Perpetua and Saturus, who each viewed paradise in visions. Executed in 203 CE, aged twenty, in her diary Perpetua describes heaven as a large garden with crowds of people dressed in white. According to Saturus, a contemporary of Perpetua, heaven is a great open space, with walls of light, roses as high as trees, and angels chanting praises to God.[112]

Another visionary, the author of the *Apocalypse of Paul,* has given us this description of heaven:

> The city is made of gold, and four rivers flow through it: rivers of milk, honey, wine and oil. On their banks grow trees with ten thousand branches bearing ten thousand clusters of fruit, and the country is bathed in light so bright it shows seven times more brightly than silver.[176]

Still another visionary, Mechthild of Magdeburg (circa 1207–1282), saw three heavens: the first is an earthly paradise, and Old Testament people like Enoch and Elijah are there; the second is like an immense domed cathedral; and third is the place where God and his palace are.[273]

As for hell, orthodox Christians view it as a ghastly crematorium. With its brimstone skies, rivers of blood, swamps of pus, and lakes of slime, hell is seen as a place where wicked souls are incinerated forever in lurid green fires.[585, 300]

It is grossly overcrowded; Francisco de Rivera, a seventeenth-century Catholic theologian, estimated that there would be 20 to 30 billion damned individuals in an area that is roughly the size of the Italian peninsula.[648] Others, however, suggested that there would be 100 million damned souls *per square mile,*[585] meaning that 30 billion damned individuals could languish in a space no larger than New York City!

Perhaps the most famous description of the infernal region is from Giovanni Pietro Pinamonti (1632–1703), whose book, *Hell Opened to Christians*, was used by James Joyce, the novelist, in *A Portrait of the Artist as a Young Man*.[448]

Pinamonti's book says that the walls of hell are four thousand miles thick. The damned are so packed into this prison that they cannot move, and they are so weak that they cannot remove the worms gnawing out their eyes. In this dreadful place, "there will be a fire, but without light."[685] According to Pinamonti:

> Every one that is damned will be like a lighted furnace, which has its own flames in itself; all that filthy blood will boil in the veins, the brains in the skull, the heart in the breast, the bowels within the unfortunate body, surrounded with an abyss of fire.[685]

Worst of all, in traditional Christianity, this torment will be forever. The Gospel of Matthew (25:4) speaks of the "everlasting fire prepared for the devil and his angels," and the Synod of Constantinople,[333] which met in 543 CE, made this declaration:

> If anyone shall say or think that there is a time limit to the torment of demons or ungodly persons, or that there will ever be an end to it, or that they will be pardoned or made whole again, let him be excommunicated.

How can the torments last forever?

In a graphic passage, Radulphus Ardens (died around 1200 CE) makes this point:

> For just as an ox tears not up the grass by the root, but so devours it that every day he may devour more, so the wicked will be forever tortured by death, and will not be annihilated, that they may forever live and forever die.[585]

THE VARIETY OF CONCEPTS OF THE AFTERLIFE

So, are afterlife concepts simple? Is it all about an immortal soul, good and evil, and eternal rewards and punishments? In fact, if we survey the entire human experience—if we look at all cultures and times—we will see a variety of opinions.

The points that follow will give the reader a glimpse of the diversity.

1. Do not assume that the death experience is the same for everyone.

According to Jainism, an ancient religion from India, if the dying person is a wise and virtuous sage, his soul will exit from the top of his head. If he is a lecher, his soul will leave through his genitals. If he is vile and wicked, his soul will exit from his anus.[503]

2. If the afterlife exists, do not assume that the dead know where they are.

According to Jewish rabbis in the Hasidic tradition, individuals that refuse to give up attachment to the physical body and the material world—and individuals who have died violently or suddenly and are unaware that they are dead—these individuals remain in *Olam ha-Tohu*, the "world of confusion." These spirits have not accepted death, and they attempt to stay in close contact with the living.[716] Such souls think that they are alive, but they are not.

Fortunately, if a soul can recognize that he is in such a state, he can escape. As one rabbi pointed out, once someone realizes that there is such a thing as the world of confusion, he is *not* in it.[716]

3. If there is an afterlife, do not assume that your initial experiences there will continue forever unchanged.

Westerners describe beautiful lights and beckoning entities in near-death experiences,[44] and they assume that they not only survive, but survive eternally in paradise.[597, 119]

In the Mahabharata, the classic Indian text, however, Yudhishthira learns that those who die with *little* sin go first to a hell to be cleansed, then to a heaven. Those who die with little virtue go first to a heaven for a brief enjoyment for their merit, and then they are cast for a long term into a hell.[139, 238]

Interestingly, in Chinese religion, heaven is not an eternal reward. To remain in a "heavenly assignment," one must continue to act in a worthy manner while in the otherworld. A shameful action could result in rebirth on earth or even demotion to a hell.[637]

4. If the afterlife exists, we may lose our minds there.

According to the Yap Islanders, who live in Micronesia in the western Pacific Ocean, the soul of the dead either becomes idiotic or it retains full possession of its wits and intelligence. Always, one or the other occurs.[900]

5. If the afterlife exists, it may be our real home.

According to the ancient Sumerians, Babylonians, and Assyrians, man's real place is the underworld. After a brief sojourn here, he will be forever there.[637]

6. If a heaven does exist, do not assume that salvation—going to a good place—is easy.

Lewis du Moulin, a devout Christian and an Oxford professor, wrote in his *Moral Reflections upon the Number of the Elect* that from the time of Adam only 1 in 100,000 would be saved, or perhaps only one in one million.[585]

In a similar vein, according to Berthold of Regensburg (circa 1210–1272), a medieval Franciscan friar, only 1 person out of every 100,000 people would be saved.[875]

Such numbers could explain why the traditional Christian heaven is so small. According to chapter 21 of the Book of Revelation, heaven is a perfect cube 12,000 furlongs on a side. Since a furlong is one-eighth of a mile, heaven is 1500 miles on each side. Resting on the planet earth, heaven would cover about one-half of the United States.

By way of comparison, Vaikuntha, the heaven of the Hindu god named Vishnu, is 80,000 miles in circumference.[932] On the other hand, the Mahabharata states that the heaven of the god named Brahma is 800 miles long, 400 miles wide, and 40 miles high.[932]

7. Do not assume that the next world will be strikingly different from this one.

The Thonga (Tsonga) people—a Bantu nation in South Africa—say that the otherworld is an exact reproduction of this one.[313]

The Chinese are so convinced that the otherworld resembles this one that they bury a type of currency with the dead. Called "spirit money," it is for buying things and paying "bribes" to bureaucrats in the next world.[4, 535]

8. Do not assume, however, that the otherworld is an ordinary world.

Eskimo and Mongol shamans agree that the land of the dead is a real place, but it is a "kind of looking-glass reversal of the world we know."[9] The same idea is found in Lapp religion. In the underworld, everything is upside down, and the soles of dead people's feet move against our own.[50]

When it is winter there, it is summer here, and when it is nighttime there, it is daylight here. When there is famine there, it means abundance here.[266] Moreover, what is broken here is whole there, and vice versa, and that is the reason grave goods and offerings are broken.[266]

In these looking-glass otherworlds, even aging can be reversed, with souls growing younger day by day as they head toward babyhood again.[268, 266]

9. If heaven exists, do not assume that you will abide there forever.

In Eastern religions such as Buddhism and Hinduism, being born in a heavenly realm is not permanent, and there is suffering when you die there. Only *nirvana* or *moksha*—the cessation of rebirth—removes all suffering.[70, 238]

10. If a heaven exists, do not assume that there is only one such realm.

Hindu texts, such as the Mahabharata, the Ramayana, and the Puranas, describe many paradise locations. In addition to Svargaloka, which is located "at the back of the sky" and is reached by ascent on "golden light,"[787, 781] there are the five heavens of the five great gods: the heaven of Indra (where we will be entertained by dancers and musicians), the heaven of Shiva (where the god and his family reign), the heaven of Vishnu (constructed from gold and covered with lotus flowers), the heaven of Krishna (with its shapely girls and devotees), and the heaven of Brahma (where souls enjoy the company of celestial nymphs).[261]

According to the Mormons (the Church of Jesus Christ of Latter Day Saints), there are three heavens: the Celestial Kingdom (reserved for pious Mormons), the Terrestrial Kingdom (for those who lived respectably but "were blinded by the craftiness of men"), and the Telestial Kingdom (for those who "received not the gospel," including "liars, and sorcerers, and adulterers, and whoremongers").[800] Interestingly, the married couples in the highest level of the Celestial Kingdom can eventually become gods and goddesses, with the husband in control of an entire universe.[74, 726]

11. If heavens exist, do not assume that they are without pain.

According to Hindu texts, entities in the heavens realize that they will one day have to leave heaven and reenter the circle of rebirth, and this causes unhappiness. In the words of the *Vishnu Purana:*

> Not in hell alone do the souls of the deceased undergo pain: there is no cessation even in heaven; for its temporary inhabitant is ever tormented with the prospect of returning to earth. Again he must be born upon the earth, and again he must die.[932, 898]

Thus, the *Markandeya Purana* says:

Likewise, there is great misery even in heaven, beginning with the very moment when people ascend there for this thought enters their minds: "I am going to hell from here."[238, 559]

12. Do not assume that a hell exists.

Hells, which tend to be underworlds, are not found among hunting cultures. Hunting cultures typically locate their afterworlds beyond the horizon or in the sky,[415] and the dead are NOT punished in those places.[4]

(The farmer, in contrast, has underworlds, and underworlds tend to be less cheerful than skyworlds.[414] Indeed, they may be places of retribution.)

13. If an underworld exists, do not assume that it is always less pleasant than an upper world.

The Greenland Eskimos, who do not believe in a hell, have two pleasant otherworlds. One, which is under the earth and the sea, is a place of sunshine, which has animals in abundance. The other afterworld, which is above the earth and under the sky, is less pleasant, and is colder, but it is still comfortable. Sometimes, when many have died at once, the souls in the latter place can be seen at night. When we see these souls, we call them the aurora borealis, or the Northern Lights.[617, 9]

According to Paul Egede (1708–1789), the Greenland Eskimos believe that men who drown and women who die during childbirth go to the underworld.[617]

14. If hell exists, do not assume that it is eternal. It may be a gruesome purgatory that ultimately ends.

According to Paramahansa Yogananda (1893–1952), a Hindu sage, because "a finite cause cannot have an infinite effect," even the greatest sinner is not damned forever.[955]

In Buddhism, although damnation can last 576 million years, it will ultimately end.[9, 176] While souls are in the Buddhist hells, they are comforted by a *bodhisattva* (an enlightened being who forgoes nirvana in order to save others). Named Ksitigarbha, by choice he wanders in the infernal regions, comforting tormented beings by his presence. He has vowed not to achieve Buddhahood until all the hells are emptied.[208, 963]

In Jainism, Mahapadma, who will be the first of the next chain of twenty-four "pathfinders," or great religious teachers, is presently burning in a hell for a crime.[249]

In the Mormon faith, Mormons teach that someone in hell can repent and escape.[74, 570]

15. If hell once existed, do not assume that it still exists.

According to the mysterious Yezidis, followers of the "Peacock Angel," the rebel angel who rebelled against Allah and now controls the world, hell no longer exists. The Peacock Angel wept for seven thousand years and extinguished the flames so that "mankind may not suffer torture."[428, 19, 274]

16. If a hellish place of punishment exists, we may be in it now.

According to the teachings of the Cathars, a persecuted religion found in Medieval Europe, this world is the realm of unhappiness and punishment, and without knowledge we continue to reincarnate here. In other words, there is no hell below this world.[304, 51]

17. If other worlds exist, they may in fact number in the billions!

According to Professor Barry Kemp, an Egyptologist, the ancient Egyptians believed that each dead individual has his own personal universe and actually is that universe.[471]

Indeed, Spell 4 of the Egyptian *Book of the Dead* assumes that a separate otherworld exists for each and every person who reaches the afterlife.[471, 126] In this personal universe, to use Kemp's words, "the ultimate authority" will be your "inner thoughts and voice."[471]

Of course, each human, while alive, already spends one-third of his life in his own world. In the words of the ancient Greek sage Heraclitus (circa 535–circa 475 BCE), "We share a world when we are awake; each sleeper is in a world of his own."[206]

Perhaps the afterlife is a continuation of that process. And, as Professor Hornell Hart (1888–1967) noted, just as the dreams of people sleeping in the same room do not invalidate or conflict with one another,[377] so we can imagine that the afterlife experiences of each person exist independently.[71]

18. If other worlds exist, they may be closer than you think.

Allan Kardec (1804–1869), the French founder of Spiritism, claimed that between reincarnations the *souls* of the dead exist on the other planets.[527, 462, 35] Such souls, of course, would be invisible to astronauts or satellite cameras.

19. If the afterlife exists, do not assume that it is spiritual in nature.

In his writings, St. Augustine (354–430 CE), the great Christian theologian, insists on resurrection of the flesh. According to Augustine, only god can exist without a body.[9]

For Christians, to use the words of Professor Jeffrey Burton Russell, "the resurrected body will be identical with our earthly body, but transfigured; it would be immune from death and sorrow; it will be at the height of its powers, free from disease and deformity and around thirty years old, the age at which Christ began his ministry."[749, 48]

20. If the resurrection of the flesh occurs, do not assume that all people are resurrected.

In his letters, Paul the "Apostle" (circa 5–circa 67 CE) never refers to the resurrection of the wicked or the resurrection of all men, but to the resurrection of believers only. According to Paul, this resurrection happens at the second coming of the Christ.[9]

Paul never speaks of hell as a place or describes its pain. He refers to sinners as "those that perish."[9]

21. Do not assume that everyone has an afterlife.

Perhaps, to use the words of P. D. Ouspensky, survival belongs only to the "higher zoological" type.[656]

According to Andrew Jackson Davis (1826–1910), the American seer, there are some individuals in every race who are *not* born on the human side, and they will not be immortal unless they cultivate the spiritual side. Specifically, Davis said that some in human form have a "quadruped brain": defiled by stupidity, they only eat, sleep, copulate, and pass waste, and they lose nothing by extinction.[216]

Likewise, the occultist and mystic George Gurdjieff (circa 1877–1949) said that ordinary people do not survive death. Only those who awaken their minds and empower their wills survive.[937, 673, 58]

So, how many do survive?

That is unclear, but Spell 152 of the Egyptian *Book of the Dead* speaks of the millions who dwell in the hereafter.[404, 126]

22. On the other hand, perhaps the afterlife is our destiny.

As Professor Anne Ross points out in *Pagan Celtic Britain,* the ancient Celts believed that the otherworld was their birthright—their natural heritage. They saw it as the "home of the gods" and the "source of all pleasure"—"a place as definite and almost as tangible as the mundane world"—and anticipated going there with joy and passion. Never did they suggest that their paradise—a place of beauty and the land of youth—was a reward for ethical behavior.[742, 794, 387]

23. Do not assume that reincarnation (that there are a limited number of souls and they return)[9] is exclusively an Asian idea.

The concept is also found in the Americas, in Africa, in Australia, and in the Arctic.[441] Indeed, "reincarnation is widespread in animistic, tribal, and shamanistic peoples throughout the world."[441, 305]

When reincarnation is found among archaic peoples, it is haphazard, and is determined by heredity, or by tribal status.[9]

When reincarnation is found in "civilizations," it takes the form of retribution. In Hinduism, for example, "as one acts and as one behaves so one becomes." In other words, if someone behaves like an animal, he becomes one in next life.[487, 9, 120, 109, 71]

24. If rebirth or reincarnation occurs, do not assume that you will be born in the future.

In Hinduism, which maintains that all time exists always, your next life may actually occur in the past. Or, your next incarnation—or your previous one for that matter—may be happening now,[442, 890] and in your current life, you may meet one of your other incarnations who is also living right now.

25. If rebirth or reincarnation occurs, we may have millions or billions or trillions of lives.

In the words of one Buddhist text, "The bones of the bodies that a man has worn in countless lives, when heaped together would form a hill far larger than the lofty summits of mountains that strike his eyes with awe."[963]

And, according to an interesting story in the *Brahmavaivarta Purana,* a Hindu text, the god Vishnu, disguised as a boy in rags, points to an army of ants and makes this observation to the god Indra:

I saw the ants, O Indra, filing in a long parade. Like you, each by virtue of pious deeds once ascended to the rank of a king of the gods. But now, through many births, each has become again an ant. This army [of ants] is an army of former Indras.[262, 108]

26. If we do indeed have millions of lives, over time everyone does everything.

As Jorge Luis Borges (1899–1986) eloquently stated:

They knew that over an infinitely long span of time, all things happen to all men. As reward for his past and future virtues, every man merited every kindness, yet also every betrayal, as reward for his past and future iniquities.[102]

And L. Ron Hubbard (1911–1986), an American writer who believed that we live trillions of lives on many worlds, made this observation: "You've been sheep, goats, spacemen, space officers. You've been governors, kings, princes, ditch-diggers, slaves, gladiators, carpenters, bricklayers, amusement-park barkers, operators. You have turned planets into parks and parks into cinders."[884]

Moreover, if, as Buddhism teaches, the cycle of rebirth is beginningless and the number of beings is vast yet finite, it is possible that each being has been in every possible relationship with every other being in the vastness of time. In the words of Professor Donald Lopez, "Every human, animal, insect, hell being, god, and ghost has been one's friend and foe, ally and adversary, protector and assistant, savior and murderer."[535]

27. If rebirth occurs, do not assume that it will ever end.

In Buddhism, the wheel of rebirth has no beginning and no end, "except for those fortunate beings who successfully traverse the path to nirvana, the state of eternal freedom from birth and death."[536]

28. If rebirth occurs, it may occur within families.

The Yoruba in western Africa believe that each person is a reincarnation of a dead ancestor.[514]

29. If you reach the next world, do not assume that you will remember your experiences here.

According to the Hindus, just as we cannot remember the previous lives that led us here, a soul in a heaven or hell realm (temporary places) may not remember how he got there.[139]

As scholar Heinrich Zimmer noted,

In the Oriental hells and heavens, though multitudes of beings are depicted in their agonies and joy, none retains the traits of his earthly personality. Some remember having been once elsewhere and know what the deed was through which the present punishment was incurred; nevertheless, all are steeped and lost in their present states.[963]

Interestingly, Professor Carl B. Becker suggests that memories of previous lives may be suppressed and forgotten because birth and death are traumatic.[71]

30. If we survive, do not assume that the personality survives.

In India, the concept of nirvana does not involve personality and personal immortality. What is promised is deliverance from transmigration or endless rebirth.[9]

On the other hand, in some of the popular religions of India and Asia—in the *bhakti* (devotional) tradition, for example—the promise is to be born in the paradise of a god such as Indra or a Pure Land of Amitabha. In such places, the individual continues.[9, 120]

31. Do not assume that the afterlife and moral behavior are connected.

According to the legendary scholar, Sir James Frazer (1854–1941), in many religions, the virtuous are not rewarded and the evil are not punished in the afterlife. In other words, "all goes on in the other world much as in this."[313]

It is significant that hunter-gatherers (the state in which the human race has spent more than 99.9 percent of its existence) do *not* connect the afterlife with morals. Only the farmers do that.

And, as Professor Gregory Shushan has pointed out, it is noteworthy that later conceptions of the afterlife—the ones that maintain that salvation is the reward for ethical behavior—seem to benefit the ruling elite. By ensuring moral behavior, they preserve the power structure of the ruling class in society.[787]

This idea is clear in the *Chandogya Upanishad*. According to this Hindu text, those whose conduct pleases the gods are born in one of the three higher castes, but those who are vile and wicked enter "a foul and stinking womb, such as that of a bitch, a pig, or an outcaste."[63, 162]

32. If ethics are a factor in survival, do not assume that virtue leads to life.

Among the Binjhwar, a Dravidian tribe in India, only the *wicked* survive death. They become malignant ghosts, while good people are simply "snuffed out."[313]

Among the fierce Dyaks of Borneo, a man's status in the next world is based on the number of human heads that he has taken in this one.[9]

It is also noteworthy that the people of San Cristoval, one of the Solomon Islands in the Pacific Ocean, believe that if a man was gentle and killed no one in life, he will become cruel and kill men after his death. People attribute mortal diseases to him.[313]

33. If ethics are a factor, understand that a certain tradition within Hinduism and Buddhism teaches that vice is one path to salvation.

Called left-handed Tantra, it is a secret teaching recorded in mysterious books written in "twilight language."[296, 826, 487]

According to left-handed Tantra, a "short path"[208] to enlightenment involves the violation of moral laws.[487] Very literally, practitioners use meat, wine, sexual orgies, excrement, and urine to achieve salvation.[204, 826]

The Tantric texts frequently repeat this saying: "By the same acts that cause some men to burn in hell for thousands of years, the yogin gains his eternal salvation."[264, 267]

And, these words appear in the *Kalarnava Tantra*:

The sensual pleasure that women provide,

The joy of wine, the taste of meat:

It's the undoing of fools,

But for the wise, the pathway to salvation.[826, 456]

Left-handed Tantra is a dangerous path, and it leads *only* the wise to freedom and bliss. Others, the unprepared, risk illness, madness, and death, and they will end up in greater bondage.[296, 208]

Since Tantric knowledge will bring disaster to those unready for it, and since there are dreadful karmic consequences for revealing Tantric secrets,[296, 487] I cannot describe it here.

I will simply note that all Tantric indulgences, including the sexual orgies, must be performed in a sacred context under the guidance of a guru (teacher). If that were not the case, according to Wolf-Dieter Storl, "any animal in rut would become enlightened."[826]

So, be warned! *Kaulavalinirnaya,* a Tantric text, says anyone who studies it without a guru will die and go to a hell.[465, 296]

34. If ethics are a factor, do not assume that innocence from "a lack of opportunity" will win salvation.

As H. L. Mencken (1880–1956) noted, most men remain faithful to their wives because of "habit, fear, poverty, lack of imagination, lack of enterprise, stupidity," and "religion," but that is *not* virtue.[583]

In the East, an innocent person—a virtuous person—is someone who is exposed to evil and remains uncorrupted.[665]

In Zen Buddhism, the classic definition of the sage is this: his mind is like a mirror that reflects the evils, horrors, and filth of the world without receiving the least stain.[92]

35. If ethics are a factor, do not assume that all human cultures and religions define virtue and crime in the same ways.

As the infamous Marquis de Sade (1740–1814) noted, in human history and prehistory, "there is no atrocity that has not been deified," and "no virtue that has not been stigmatized."[225]

On one hand, the Jains of India teach that causing harm to a sentient being is a hideous crime.[534] They will not "injure, abuse, oppress, enslave, insult, torment, torture, or kill any creature or living thing."[23]

Thus, the Jain sage does not pick fruit from a tree (that hurts the tree), but he eats fruit that has fallen to the ground.[715] Pious Jains will not even speak the truth if it harms others. Instead, they remain silent.[23]

In contrast, in many traditional religions, especially in cultures that emphasize bravery, courage, and individual initiative,[415] violence is a "form of worship or religious activity."[618, 131] To *Homo necans* (man the killer), hunting animals and slaying humans are consecrated actions.[618]

Thus, among the nineteenth-century American Indians, violence was endorsed: torture and sacrifice in the East, scalping (a fatal operation) on the Plains, headhunting in the Northwest.[618] Professor Jesse Nash, in his remarkable "No More War Parties: The Pacification and Transformation of Plains Indian Religion," offers valuable information on these beliefs.

36. If ethics are a factor, it may be possible to evade the rules.

The Egyptian afterlife has a last judgment, but Spell 125 of the Egyptian *Book of the Dead* has one purpose: to "magically" outflank the last judgment.[261, 41]

37. If the afterlife is not determined by how you live, it may be connected with how you die.

According to the Erave, a Melanesian people in the Pacific Ocean, the warriors who die in battle (and the women who supported them) go to the "Red Place" in the sky and become sky-dwellers. All others go to the "Place of Brown" on earth.[867]

Likewise, the Aztec afterlife, writes Professor Miguel Leon-Portilla in *Aztec Thought and Culture,* "was determined not on the basis of conduct in life, but by the nature of his death."

Warriors who die in battle, people who are offered as human sacrifices, and women who die in childbirth go to the sun, a place of honor.[523]

Anyone who dies from drowning, lightning, or dropsy (a water disease) goes to Tlalocan, a paradise of Tlaloc, the god of rain.[523, 312]

Babies who died while still nursing go to Chichiualquauitl, the Land of the Breast Tree. This place has a huge tree covered with beautiful breasts.[718, 171, 787]

Finally, those who die from all other causes (such as old age) go to Mictlan, the "emerald realm," a putrid underworld.[787, 523] This is ruled by Mictlancihuatl and his woman Micteca. These gods drink pus from a human skull.[718]

38. Realize that the afterlife may exist even if gods do not.

As Sir James Frazer pointed out, some cultures do not believe in god (a fact Charles Darwin liked to emphasize[205]), but all cultures ever found believe in ghosts.[312, 585]

In fact, Gerard van der Leeuw (1890–1950), the Dutch scholar, noted that "God was a latecomer in the history of religion."[42]

39. Do not assume that you cannot become a god or a goddess.

In Hinduism, as the great Joseph Campbell (1904–1987) noted, reincarnation is a "basic law," and deities are simply "beings (formerly human or animal) who had merited bliss." Ultimately, "when the merit expired their high seats were vacated to other candidates and they descend again into human, animal, or even demonic forms."[963]

In other words, there is always a god named Indra, but different souls will be reborn as Indra. (Interestingly, the Buddhists claim that the Buddha was born twenty times as the god Indra and four times as the god Brahma.)[901, 963]

How many gods are there? According to the *Linga Purana* of the Hindus, "there are two hundred and eighty million gods," and, during "the cycles of humanity," the number of gods increases to "three billion, nine hundred and twenty million."[204, 532]

In the religion of Jainism, another ancient Indian religion that teaches we may become gods, there are more deities than humans in the universe![184]

The Jain universe, which is "uncreated" and eternal,[184] contains four levels of existence: gods, humans, animals-plants-minerals, and "hellish beings."[184] Humans, to use the words of Professor John E. Cort, "constitute demographically the smallest of these states. There are many more infernal and celestial beings. By far the largest category is that of plants-and-animals."[184]

40. If you come back as a god, remember that you may later go to a hell.

In Eastern lore, gods are higher than we are—they have greater longevity, beauty, and freedom from pain—but ultimately their charms wither, their fragrance turns to stench, and gods who focused on pleasure will fall, perhaps into hell. In the words of one Tibetan lama, "Many long-lived gods are fools."[665]

According to the *Linga Purana,* the life span of a god is 4,320,000 human years.[204, 532]

41. If gods exist, do not assume that they can save you.

The all-powerful and authoritarian god, a feature of many modern religions, is a relatively recent idea. According to philosopher Charles Hartshorne, in his *Omnipotence and Other Theological Mistakes,* omnipotence or the "tyrant ideal of power" (the despot "magnified to infinity") was developed by Western minds in the Dark or Middle Ages. In fact, in most religions, gods are limited beings. Hunting cultures, for example, are egalitarian, and because hunters have no autocratic chief, the idea of a ruling deity, a "Great Spirit," is meaningless to them.[881]

According to the philosopher Epicurus (341–270 BCE), the gods may be simply entities that share the universe with us. It is possible, Epicurus said, that the gods are creatures who live blessed and untroubled lives among the stars without bothering humans or even taking interest in us.[360, 294]

Curiously, in ancient Greek religion, the Olympian gods avoid the dead. In the play *Hippolytus,* by Euripides (circa 480–406 BCE), the Olympians may not "look at the dead or to sully their eyes with the expirations of the dying."[330]

For the pagans of Celtic Ireland, the deities (called Sid, Sidh, or Sidhe) are master magicians, but they are not all-powerful beings. In the

"Adventure of Nera," the warrior Nera and his companions wait until Samhain night (Hallowe'en), when the realm of "all the Sid of Ireland are open," and they attack the gods and carry off some of the divine loot![794]

In the *Iliad* of Homer, Diomedes, a human, wounds Aphrodite and Ares with his spear.[130]

In the Aztec universe, gods and humans occupy the same cosmos with other beings. Gods have power that we do not possess, but they do not hold complete power over humans.[718, 671]

For the Indians of North America, there is no sharp distinction between gods and humans and humans and animals.[413, 293]

And, in modern Gardnerian witchcraft (the tradition promulgated by Gerald Gardner (1884–1964), British scholar of magic), the goddesses and gods need human aid and are not all-powerful.[328]

42. On the other hand, in Hinduism, any contact with a god might benefit your afterlife.

In one Hindu account, Kitava (his name means "rogue") stumbled while bringing flowers to his "whore." As he fell, Kitava uttered a curse and cried out, "Shiva!"

For offering flowers to the god Shiva (that was not Kitava's actual intention), not only was he saved from hell, but he was given the throne of Indra, the king of the gods.

Eventually, he would be reborn as Bali, an anti-god, but that, as professor Wendy Doniger has pointed out, is another story.[238]

43. Do not be surprised to learn that in some traditions, even hating a god can have merit.

Very literally, in Hinduism, reviling a god can help you. According to the *Bhagavata Purana,* a sacred Hindu text devoted to Vishnu, any contact with this god, *even hatred,* can lead to paradise. In the words of the text: "Desire, hatred, fear, or love toward the lord, filling the heart with devotion, destroy all sins and bind one to the lord."[643, 296, 81]

When you hate something, you are still focused on it, so the Hindus maintain that someone who hates a god is spiritually superior to someone who never thinks about god at all.[238]

This, of course, reminds us of a biblical passage (Revelation 3:15-16): "I would thou wert cold or hot. So then because thou art lukewarm, and neither cold nor hot, I will spew thee out of my mouth."

44. If gods exist—and if they determine the placement of individuals in the other worlds—do not assume that they follow modern standards of ethics.

As classicist Walter Burkert noted, there is "no devil in the ancient religions, but each god has his dark and dangerous side."[130]

In one Greek myth, Zeus rapes his mother (Rhea-Demeter) and sires Persephone. He then rapes Persephone (in the form of a snake) and sires Dionysus.[130, 354]

The Old Testament god, meanwhile, massacres children, annihilates cities, and orders the execution of sodomites (his harsh activities are detailed in my short work, *The Crimes of Jehovah*). The New Testament god does seem nicer, but in the Book of Revelation, when Jesus is separating saints and sinners (the sheep and the goats) at the end times, the wrathful side reappears.[803, 15, 307]

What does all of this mean?

In short, do NOT assume that gods prefer pacifists to jihadists.

45. If gods exist—and if they are involved in this world and the afterworlds—do not assume that their choices are based on reason and fairness.

When the Hindu mystic named Ramakrishna (1836–1886) achieved enlightenment, he saw that the universe is a game, and he laughed.[113] He said: "The Divine Mother is always sportive and playful. This universe is her play. She is self-willed and must always have her way. She is full of bliss. She gives freedom to one out of a hundred thousand."[963]

When asked why the goddess does not free everyone from endless rebirths, Ramakrishna replied: "That is her will. She wants to continue playing with her created beings . . . . Her pleasure is in continuing the game."[963]

46. Do not assume that if you survive death that you survive forever.

Although many religions talk of immortal souls—and Socrates, in *Phaedrus,* says "the soul" is "imperishable"[9, 690]—whatever remains of a man after death may *not* last forever. It may linger only for a time, as smoke lingers after a fire is extinguished.[544]

According to the Aztecs, the soul of the *average* person (someone who died from natural causes) exists only four years after death, and then disappears.[13, 718, 9, 787, 226]

According to the Dyaks in Borneo, the soul has seven lives, after which it is annihilated.[336]

47. On the other hand, according to Hindu texts, we are forever.

As Krishna says to the warrior prince Arjuna, in the Bhagavad Gita: "If any man thinks he slays, and if another thinks he is slain, neither knows the way of truth. The eternal in man cannot kill: the eternal in man cannot die."

Indeed, in the Bhagavad Gita, Krishna teaches the warrior Arjuna that we have always existed and will always exist: "There never was a time when I and thou were not in existence, and all these princes too. Nor will the day come, hereafter, when all of us will cease to be."[963, 80]

According to Krishna, although bodies come to an end, "he who is clothed in the body is eternal, indestructible, and infinite."[963, 80, 464, 273, 139]

48. If the afterlife is real, do not assume that it is a destination. In fact, the afterlife may be an endless journey.

The Hasidic rabbi Yehiel Mikhal of Zlotchov (1721–1786), who appeared to one of his disciples in spectral form years after his own death, described his experience:

Know, that from the moment I died, I have been wandering from world to world. And the world which yesterday was spread over my head as the Garden of Eden, is today the earth under my feet, and the Garden of Eden of today is the earth of tomorrow.[716]

In Egyptian paganism, the journey through the otherworld with its obstacles is one of the central themes of the *Book of the Dead,* but there is no final destination. According to Egyptologist Barry Kemp, the otherworld is not a place of blissful peace, but after death we move from point to point forever.[471]

49. If souls exist, do not assume that everyone has a soul.

The Tinneh Indians of Canada say their "medicine" has no power over white men because "white men have no souls."[415]

According to the Tenino people, Native Americans who occupied a territory in what is now Oregon, embryos and babies have no souls.[415]

The Cherokee people say that children have no souls.[415]

50. Finally, do not assume that you need a soul to survive death.

Theravada Buddhism, which is found in south Asia, teaches rebirth, but denies that there is a soul.

According to the Theravada Buddhist doctrine of *anatta* (no soul), there is no enduring entity that persists from one life to the next. At the death of one personality, a new one comes into being, much as the flame of a dying candle can serve to light the flame of another.[305]

It is a Buddhist idea that an individual's desire to live—as distinct from his mind and personality—could survive death.[208]

Or, to paraphrase P. D. Ouspensky, what survives is the person's last thought.[656]

IV
Souls and Other Worlds
Some Interesting Traditions

My soul is from elsewhere, I am sure of that, and I intend to end up there.

JALAL AL-DIN AL-RUMI

Crazy Horse dreamed and went into the world where there is nothing but the spirits of all things. That is the real world that is behind this one, and everything we see here is something like a shadow from that one.

BLACK ELK
(OGLALA SIOUX)

In Ireland this world and the world we go to after death are not far apart.

W. B. YEATS

It is not born, nor does it die. It has not come from anywhere, has not become anyone. Unborn, everlasting, eternal, primeval, it is not slain when the body is slain.

KATHA UPANISHAD

In this section, when archaic religions are discussed, they are examined in their pristine state. Sadly, because of the missionaries of the monotheistic faiths (Red Jacket, a chief of the Senecas, called them the "Black Coats"),[157] some of these religions have been destroyed or altered.

THE SOUL CONCEPT

Widespread, and Widely Varying

Although Buddhism denies that there are souls, most religions embrace the concept.

Indeed, the Japanese believe that tools that are more than a hundred years old *acquire* souls, and that is the reason that the prudent Japanese destroy old tools.[743]

Although most Westerners (if they believe in souls) think each person has one soul, most polytheistic cultures believe that each person has multiple souls.[671, 519, 415, 266] According to Professor Gregory Shushan, humans experiencing out-of-body experiences produced the idea of multiple souls: one soul must stay and keep the body alive while the "free soul" travels.[787]

Thus, the Polar Eskimo say that our body soul—which keeps us alive—is in our breath and warmth. Our free soul—which can wander—is our shadow.[415]

In many religions, souls are considered immaterial and otherworldly—the Hindu Upanishads, in a beautiful passage, describe the soul as a being of light resembling a smokeless flame[787, 883]—but that is not always the case.

In some traditions, the soul has an element of physicality. Thus, the Orans of Bengal sprinkle ashes on the floor to look for the footprints of the dead.[9] The Aztecs, to track otherworldly beings, spread corn flour.[336]

Interestingly, Duncan MacDougall, an early twentieth-century physician, carefully weighed six dying people under controlled conditions, and he found that the soul weighed three-quarters of an ounce, or twenty-one grams.[350, 734] MacDougall published his findings in *American Medicine,* a prestigious journal, in 1907.[543]

THE SOUL IN ABORIGINAL AUSTRALIA

We Never Leave This World

The traditional Aboriginal people of central Australia inhabit a harsh desert. In their pre-contact state, they had no clothes, no metals, no agriculture, and no bows and arrows.[179, 312] Living in archaic promiscuity, they had no idea that sexual intercourse causes birth.[811, 292] They had never seen water boil and they counted only to three.[945, 867]

But, these intrepid hunters and gatherers survived in areas where British settlers perished from hunger and thirst.[837] Among their inventions was the return boomerang.[179] Viewed as the perfect magical weapon, it has speed, can fly, can kill at a distance, and can return to the hunter's hand.

In contrast to the Abrahamic faiths—where god the omnipotent is a tyrant and man the sinner is a criminal—the Aboriginals have a religion that is beautiful in its simplicity.

Like the people of ancient Egypt,[926] the Aboriginals believe there is no natural death. Creatures do not die—they are killed. The violence is either direct—as in a spear thrust—or indirect—as in the sorcery that causes sickness.[336]

Sir George Grey (1812–1898), describing the people, made this observation: "The natives do not allow that there is such a thing as a death from natural causes; they believe, that were it not for murderers or the malignity of sorcerers, they might live forever."[312]

Because every death is a murder, every death requires vengeance. To find the killer, the closest relative must sleep with his head on the corpse, and the murderer is identified in a dream.[312, 72] Or, if the dead man is cremated, the relatives walk in the direction of the smoke and kill the first person that they encounter.[312]

Interestingly, in the Central Australian religion, which is tens of thousands of years old, evil is absent as a religious concept. (Curiously innocent, men of the Walibri tribe in central Australia greet by shaking each other's penises.)[837] People and ancestors can perform bad actions, but they are not evil.[837]

The Central Australians have no gods and no rewards and punishments after death. They do believe in the existence of souls, however.[312]

The soul, they believe, is the size of a grain of sand. It survives death, and haunts its native land. Waiting to be reborn, the soul visits places where its ancestors camped. It will linger there until it is reborn.[312]

There is no general gathering place of the dead. Souls of each clan gather at one place, and each clan has its own place.[312]

These spirit places, which are on the earth, may be a few square yards in size or many miles.[312] They are not ordinary places, for the souls of the dead like to lurk in spectacular locations, like deep gorges or pools of water.[312]

Ultimately, all souls of the dead will enter women—through their navels—and they will make them pregnant. Souls may enter any woman, but they prefer young women.[312]

Note that in the Aboriginal mind, life comes from the land, not from the father or the mother. When a soul enters a woman, she carries life from a site.[837]

Note also that, according to the Aboriginal people of central Australia, everyone on earth is the reincarnation of a dead person who lived a long or short time ago.[312, 336] Although individual personalities do not endure, the soul does survive.[837]

FIJIAN RELIGION

All Things Survive

In the traditional religion of Fijians, a fierce Melanesian people in the Pacific, there are two souls: a dark soul (the shadow, which leaves during the night) and a light soul (the reflection in a mirror or in a body of water).[336] At death, the dark soul goes to the otherworld, while the light soul stays near the site where the death or the killing occurred.[312]

Fijians extend the afterlife not only to all humans, but also to animals, plants, and even minerals. If a human or an animal dies, the dark soul goes to a place called Bolotoo. If a stone is broken, its soul goes there. If an ax is broken, its soul goes there.[312]

Fijians have a large hole in one of their islands, and they say that in that hole you can see the souls of men, animals, plants, canoes, tools, and so forth.[312]

Note that the Melanesian perspective is lateral rather than vertical. For the people of Fiji (like the Etruscans of ancient Italy[437]), the spirit realm is somewhere on this world.[867]

Fijians believe that people have the same mental and physical faculties that they had at the hour of death.[312] In other words, as we leave this world, so we are in the next world. Old people are old there and young people are young there.[312, 935]

According to traditional Fijians, there is no retribution and no reward in the afterlife. They view going from life to death as going from pain to paradise.[312]

As a warlike people, the Fijians think that shedding blood is "no crime, but a glory." The man who kills, even if he kills a child or an old woman by ambush, is called a Koroi, a term of respect.[312, 935]

In this world and the next, however, a man who never killed lacks status.

And, like all warrior societies, the Fijians believe that the mightier a man is in life, the more dangerous he will be in death.[139, 320]

JUDAISM

Hell Lasts Only Twelve Months

According to Jewish rabbis, the process of death is quite simple. The angel of death, sometimes called the "Venom of God,"[827] will appear and place one drop of gall into the victim's mouth.[854] The victim's face will turn greenish—the color of gall—and soon his body will begin to stink.[6, 716]

Although the Torah (the first five books of the Bible and the holiest scripture of Judaism) does not specifically mention an afterlife, the Talmud (commentary on the Torah by rabbis) and the Kabbalah (Jewish occultism and mysticism) discuss the concept at length.[716]

According to the rabbis, who focused on the fate of the Jewish people *only,* after death both the body and the soul undergo physical torment for the sins committed in life.[716]

In the "judgment of the grave," which refers to the punishment of the body, the dead sinner literally feels the worms and grisly process of decomposition.[716]

To hasten decomposition and abbreviate the suffering of their loved ones, pious Jews will bury the dead in a wooden coffin bored with holes. The coffin must have no metal parts and no nails. A bag of earth (ideally from the Mount of Olives) is placed on top of the body. The corpse, wrapped in plain linen, must never be embalmed.[702, 712]

According to the rabbis, additional suffering occurs when the soul goes to a hellish realm called Gehenna. Nahmanides (1194–1270 CE), a Jewish scholar, wrote that Gehenna was created by God on the second day of creation, the only day that the Bible does not call "good."[585]

Rabbi Jeremiah bar Eleazar (flourished in the second century CE) claimed that Gehenna has three gates: one is in a wilderness, one in a sea, and one in the city of Jerusalem.[716] Gehenna is located at the left hand of god.[847, 716]

Rabbi Joshua ben Levi (first half of the third century CE), reputedly the only person to escape death at the hands of the Angel of Death,[526] visited Gehenna in the company of Elijah the prophet. According to the rabbi, Gehenna is filled with rivers of fire and pits of brimstone.[723] People burn in the fire six days each week, but the fires do not burn on the Sabbath.[965, 716] On that holy day, the souls are taken to two mountains of snow for comfort. When the Sabbath ends, they return to the fire.[585]

According to the Zohar and the Talmud, the "the punishment of the wicked in Gehenna is twelve months."[965, 716, 291] Like the punishment of the body, the punishment of the soul is limited. After spending twelve months in Gehenna, the "sinner is forgiven from all his iniquities, and like an arrow from a bow he is flung forth from Gehenna."[847, 716]

There are a *handful* of exceptions—the Talmud and the Zohar indicate that a few Jews will languish forever in a place called Tzoah

Rotakhat ("Boiling Filth" or "Boiling Feces" or "Boiling Semen")—but that is rare. The exceptions seem to number three kings and four private men.[850, 965, 849]

Ultimately, the rabbis believe that virtually all Jews will enjoy the mercy of their god. In the words of the Zohar:

> The body is punished in the grave and the soul in the fire of Gehenna for the appointed period. When this is completed she rises from Gehenna purified of her guilt like iron purified in the fire, and she is carried to the Lower Garden of Eden.[965, 716]

The Garden of Eden, of course, is a paradise.[716, 965]

Although reincarnation is not found in the Torah or the Talmud, the concept is found in the Jewish Kabbalah.[716] In the Kabbalah, the soul does not stay in the Garden of Eden forever, but goes to Tzror ha-hayyim, the "storehouse of souls," and prepares for rebirth. The Kabbalah calls reincarnation *gilgul* or "wheel."[716]

So, for the Jewish soul, it is Gehenna and purgation, then the bliss of the Garden of Eden, and then reincarnation into another life.[716]

Eventually, however, when the Messiah comes, he will bring peace and prosperity to this world, and the Jewish dead will experience a physical resurrection. They will return to life here. According to *Genesis Rabbah,* a Talmud text, "the resurrection is reserved for Israel."[846]

JAINISM

Even an Insect May One Day Become Omnipotent

Jainism is a fascinating religion from India. According to the Jains, the eternal truths of their religion are lost and rediscovered again and again in beginningless and endless time by wise sages called pathfinders. One great pathfinder was Mahavira (dates unknown, but perhaps 540–468 BCE).[534]

According to the Jains, everything that exists has a soul.[261] Not only gods, humans, and hellish beings, but also animals, plants, stones, drops of water, and so forth.[261] The Jains believe that life-forms exist even in fire.[249]

In Jainism, as in most Indian traditions, there is no such thing as a special *human* soul. There is, say the Jains, only a soul *temporarily* in a human form.[534] The soul in you now may have formerly animated a dung fly, an eagle, or a god.

In Jainism, the soul is called a *jiva. Jiva* means "alive."[715]

The jiva is pure consciousness without form or substance.[249] The jiva expands and contracts to fit the body into which it is born, like the light of a lamp expands or contracts according to the size of the room.[249, 120]

Each jiva is uncreated and imperishable. Each soul has always existed and will always exist in a universe that is without a beginning and without an end.[963, 184]

The vast but finite universe—where all rebirth takes place and where all beings exist (from gods to worms to hellish beings)—is called the *loka*. Some texts say that the loka is 14 *ropes* from top to bottom.[249] A rope (*rajju*), a unit of measurement, is the distance covered by a god flying for six months at a speed of ten million miles per second.[249]

Each soul is individual and distinctive. It is *not* part of an "oversoul."[534] The soul will never lose its individuality.[715]

In its liberated form, each jiva is omniscient, endowed with infinite energy, and is full of bliss.[963]

From beginningless time, however, souls are weighed down by *ajiva*.[534] (There is no "fall from an Eden" in Jainism.)[534] *Ajiva* means "not soul," or, more literally, "not alive."[715] All souls, throughout their beginningless existence, have been bound by this ajiva.[534]

The ajiva that diminishes the soul is called *karma*. The Jains, unlike other Indian religions such as Hinduism, view karma as a material substance.[249, 120] This karma, say the Jains, adheres to the soul and keeps it wandering from lifetime to lifetime.[534]

According to the Jains, all physical, vocal, and mental activities cause karma.[715] All actions, whether these actions are conscious or unconscious, good, evil, or morally neutral, loving or hate-filled, produce karma. Even spiritual actions, such as prayer, and physical functions, such as breathing, generate karma.[715] (In contrast, the Bhagavad Gita of Hinduism teaches that actions performed without desire have no karmic effects.)[80, 238]

According to the Jains, karma obscures knowledge, erodes perception, and corrupts the state of bliss.[715]

Because of karma, the soul remains embodied. It moves through animal life, the vegetable state, mineral life, the human realm, and the invisible realms of deities and hell beings.[715]

Some souls will remain in the cycle of rebirth forever. They are called the *abhavya*. At no point in the limitless future will they obtain liberation. They will stay in unending rebirth.[249] Time will never end and neither will their endless journeys.

Some souls, however, will escape rebirth by eliminating all defiling karmic matter. By eliminating karma, they will escape physical and intellectual limitations.[715]

To achieve this liberation, note that the Jain must eliminate *all* karma. He must obviously stop bad actions that darken his jiva,[139] but he must also stop good actions as well. Good actions whiten the soul, but good karma also keeps us in rebirth.[963]

To stop the influx of karma, the Jain must abstain from all actions, bad as well as good.[963, 120] To burn off the karma he already has, he must practice ruthless austerities, such as eating no formal meals, surviving on only the remains of the meals of others.[139, 963]

The Jain monk must practice "ascetic aloofness." By showing indifference to pleasure and pain, by showing indifference to all things, whether they are desirable, repugnant, or dangerous, his ascetic aloofness burns off karma.[963]

In the words of one Jain text:

As a large pond, when its influx of water has been blocked, dries up gradually through consumption of the water and evaporation, so the karmic material of a monk, which has been acquired through millions of births, is annihilated by austerities—provided there is no further influx.[139]

Western religions want, to use the words of Professor Zimmer, a "perfected humanity," but the Jains do not seek this. They seek "perfect non-activity."[963]

Through perfect non-activity, the jiva becomes pure and transparent like crystal. (The Jains say that all karmic material colors the soul.)[963] Sterilized of the dead material called karma, the jiva rises to the top of the loka or universe.[963] Although the liberated jiva remains in the universe, he is beyond the gods and their heavens and their powers and their pleasures.[261]

The jiva has entered Siddha-loka. "Pure, luminous, perfect,"[963] he will exist forever as an independent entity in the Abode of Perfection.[184]

Superior to a god (gods are still subject to death and rebirth),[715] the liberated jiva will never again experience death. It will become a trans-god, a being beyond god.

Pure and free and unfettered, the liberated soul or trans-god will experience the four infinities: unlimited knowledge, unlimited perception, unlimited bliss, and unlimited power.[184, 534] When it escapes the karmic cycle, the liberated jiva will retain its individuality.[715]

To achieve such a state, an individual must depend only on his own efforts. No god can help. In the grand scheme of things, say the Jains, man is isolated and independent, and he is fully in control of his destiny. In the words of the *Acaranga Sutra,* "Man, it is you who are your only friend. Why do you want a friend other than yourself?"[249]

He is alone, but a man, without the assistance of a god, can become greater than a god.

And, ironically, to become a trans-god, a sentient being that is *now* a god must first be reborn as a human. According to the Jains, rebirth as a human is the only way to enlightenment.[715]

HOMER'S GREEKS

Only the Dreamer Survives

According to the ancient Greeks of Homer's era, man lives in two worlds: the world of work and the world of sleep. Each of these two worlds has its own logic and its own limitations. There is no reason to assume that one world is more significant than the other.[237]

Modern Westerners assume that, if a person survives, it is the person in the world of work who survives death. But, according to the Homeric Greeks, the person you are now, the person who is awake and alert and living in this world, will not survive death.

What will survive, however, is the person you are in the world of sleep. In a sense, every time you sleep is a dress rehearsal for the afterlife.

How can this be?

In the *Iliad* and the *Odyssey,* each living man has several souls. Some of these souls are "body souls." They provide warmth, life, movement, and *waking* consciousness.[111] They will not survive forever.

In addition to the body souls, according to the Homeric Greeks, each man has one dream soul. The Greeks called it a *psyche,* the Greek word for "butterfly."[111]

During life, the dream soul has a spiritual existence of its own and is able to leave the body during "swoons" and sleep. Dreams, very literally, are the activity of the absent soul.[336] (Such an idea is widespread, and a Kwakiutl shaman from British Columbia called dreams "the news that is told by the souls when they come back to us."[415])

The dream soul sleeps when the body is awake. When the body is asleep, however, the dream soul is awake, and it can travel elsewhere in this world or the otherworld while the body rests in bed.[336]

Or, to use the words of Jorge Luis Borges, "That while asleep here, we are awake somewhere else, so that every man is in fact two men."[102]

Thus, Iamblichus (circa 245–circa 325 CE) states, in *Theurgia; Or The Egyptian Mysteries,* "The night time of the body is the daytime of the soul."[336, 422]

During life, the psyche of the sleeper may go to other realms and even perform tasks.[336] For the ordinary person, these "out-of-body travels" are random or haphazard. The especially gifted person, however, can direct his psyche and visit various "twilight zones."

Thus, Epimenides, a Cretan prophet and magician who lived in the sixth or seventh century before Christ, could dispatch his spirit elsewhere for knowledge and could recall it at will.[336] Likewise, Hermotimus (circa sixth century BCE) could send forth his soul to explore distant regions until his wife cremated his body.[336]

Because the Homeric psyche operated independently—outside the body—it is literally a second self, an alter ego.[738] According to Professor Erwin Rohde, the idea that the psyche "should dwell within the living and fully conscious personality, like an alien and a stranger," may seem strange to us, but this is what so-called savage peoples, all over the world, actually believe.[738]

At the end of life, the psyche, which has left the body every night, will now leave the body forever. Exiting from the mouth, the chest, a bloody wound, or the limbs,[111] the psyche journeys to Hades[111] (or Aides), an invisible place.[825]

This Homeric Hades is NOT a hell; it is NOT a place of fire, brimstone, muck, and dung.[444] It is simply a featureless land of the dead,[111] and its only vegetation is the weed named asphodel.[483, 585]

Homer's poems, as Professor Rohde points out in his writings, clearly have no idea of retribution in the afterlife. The perjurer alone suffers punishment at the hand of the gods, the punishment that he had invoked upon himself while swearing his oath.[738]

THE DRUZE

Heaven Is Ruling the World

Called the "Unitarian religion," the Druze faith is a mysterious creed that grew out of Shia Islam.[78]

The Druze believe in one god, and they believe in the successive manifestations of God in a *human* form.[395] The Druze point out that if

God could speak to the Jewish Moses in a "dry bush," why could he not speak to the faithful in the shape of a man?[395]

The Druze believe that al-Hakim, a Fatimid Caliph, is the last and greatest of these divine incarnations. Born in 985 CE, al-Hakim went for a walk outside Cairo in 1023 CE and never returned. His enemies claim that he was murdered, but the Druze deny that he died and they expect his return.[395]

(Christians associate al-Hakim with the destruction of the "Holy Sepulcher" in Jerusalem, and orthodox Muslims view him as an insane heretic and a tyrant.)[395, 333, 78]

Curiously, no one has been admitted to the Druze faith for a millennium. In 1031 CE, "the door of the Unitarian religion was closed," and from that point on, no one could enter or leave the Druze faith. Believing that new converts might betray the cause to persecutors, Baha-al-Din, a Druze leader, adopted this policy as a measure of safety. The Druze religion became wholly hereditary—a sacred privilege—a priceless treasure.[395]

The doctrines of the Druze have been secret since 1043 CE. They are shared only with trained Druze called the Uggal, or the "enlightened."[78]

Regular Druze, known as Juhhal (the "ignorant" or "uninitiated") are not given access to the six holy books or knowledge of their contents. Instead, they are given a simple form of faith and strict rules of ethical behavior.[78]

Outsiders have tried to learn Druze secrets—and they have stolen copies of the Druze scriptures—but Druze sacred writings are so esoteric that they are not "easily discernible to the uninitiated reader."[78]

It appears, however, that the Druze believe that all souls were made at the same time, and they believe that all are reborn constantly. At creation, the number of souls of believers and unbelievers was fixed.[78]

In particular, the Druze believe that the Druze are reborn as Druze. When one Druze dies, another Druze is born immediately.[78]

Rebirth, according to the Druze, is *not* based on moral behavior. "For the Druze what one does in this life has little or no bearing on the next."[638]

Interestingly, the Druze say there is no paradise and no hell. Instead, at the time of the triumphal return of al-Hakim, there will be a complete victory of the Unitarian religion on earth. With that victory, the Druze will become the ruling class—an elite—and they will be rewarded with high worldly offices.[395]

As for unbelievers and renegades, when al-Hakim returns, they will be given hard and menial labor. They will become a servile class.[395]

EMANUEL SWEDENBORG, CHRISTIAN SEER

We Become What We Love

Aleister Crowley (1875–1947), a modern arch-blasphemer, a man who proudly called himself the "Beast," and who once baptized a toad— giving it the name of Jesus—and then crucified it,[153, 563] said that he had no interest in heaven. The self-proclaimed Beast, infamous for his sexual depravities, viewed hell as a masochist delight, a place where he could enjoy torments at the hands of violent, whorish women, and that was the destination that he desired.[563]

If the teachings of Emanuel Swedenborg (1688–1772) are correct, Crowley, who died in 1947, got his wish.[501]

According to Swedenborg—a Swedish scientist who, at the age of fifty-six, began to have detailed visions of other worlds—there is one God, Jesus, and he does not send anyone to heaven or to hell.[841]

Instead, the dead "lead the same kind of life they had led in the world," and those who enjoy virtue and charity will do those things in the next world. Those who like crime and violence will continue those sins after death.[840]

They will do these things forever because "after death we remain the same forever in regard to our volition or dominant love."[840] Our dominant love—love of God, love of other people, love of knowledge, love of power, love of gold—this love "never changes to eternity" because "we are our love."[840]

After death this ruling love draws us to other persons with the same ruling love. Why is that? Because, declared Swedenborg, "the only things that feel pleasant to us are the things that we love." In the afterlife, people freely associate according to their dominant love, hellish or heavenly, and they cluster into communities.[840]

Wicked people "take up with people who are devoted to similar evils,"[840] and the hells contain violent, perverted, and selfish people who enjoy crime and treachery. In hell are "crude huts, sometimes grouped in something like a city, with alleyways and streets." There are constant quarrels in hell. It is a place of violence, hostility, sexual crime, and thievery.[840]

Swedenborg even claimed that he saw a community of dead free-thinking atheist scientists in hell: they were giving lectures promoting nihilism, ridiculing the idea of god, and denying that there is an afterlife.[840]

Swedenborg emphasized that hell is not a prison. Evil people are not cast into hell—no force is involved—those in hell choose to be there. Just as carrion birds rush with delight toward rotting corpses, so the wicked will find pleasure in hell.[840, 841]

Meanwhile, in the heavens, good people will also cluster. The heavens, wrote Swedenborg, contain kind and loving people who live in houses, form communities, and even organize governments. The heavens are beautiful places with beautiful people.[840, 841]

ALFRED T. SCHOFIELD

The Dead Are in Our Universe and Are Only Inches Away

Most people believe that we live in a universe of three dimensions only. They think that all space is visible and objects here are solids with length, breadth, and height.[656]

But, as the mathematician Georg Friedrich Bernhard Riemann (1826–1866) pointed out, there may be a fourth dimension in *space*.[454] That would mean that side by side with us, there is a direction "unknown and unknowable" to us, and some other space that we are "unable to see and into which we cannot pass."[656, 393, 3, 744, 745, 393]

Oddly, people here cannot hide from entities from the fourth dimension. Even if we were to seal ourselves in windowless rooms, they could see us, hear us, and touch us. If they spoke to us from the fourth dimension, we would hear them.[744]

Although we cannot of our own power enter the fourth dimension, entities from that dimension can appear and disappear suddenly in our space. Significantly, that is how the resurrected Jesus behaved—in chapter 20 of the Gospel of John, he abruptly appeared in a closed room—and that is how the mysterious hand behaves in chapter 5 of the Book of Daniel.

These are the words of the Book of Daniel (5:5-6):

> Suddenly the fingers of a human hand appeared and wrote on the plaster of the wall, near the lampstand in the royal palace. The king watched the hand as it wrote. His face turned pale and he was so frightened that his knees knocked together and his legs gave way.

Interestingly, many theorists, including the Christian writer A. T. Schofield (1846–1929), have suggested that the dead (and God) are simply in the fourth dimension of our universe.[769] Right now, very literally, the dead may be adjacent to you. Perhaps, as L. Ron Hubbard (1911–1986) wrote, "Death is eight inches below life."[884]

We can never, by our own power, leave our own dimension or world for the other dimension, but perhaps we go there automatically when we die.

V

The Trek of Souls

Accounts of the Death Journey

Mortals waken from the dream of death with bodies unseen by those who think that they bury the body.

MARY BAKER EDDY

Death, far from being the end of the individual, is the beginning of the individual in his most formidable aspect.

C. E. VULLIAMY,
IMMORTALITY: FUNERARY RITES AND CUSTOMS

When we die we are still alive and just as human as ever.

EMANUEL SWEDENBORG,
*HEAVEN AND ITS WONDERS AND HELL:
FROM THINGS HEARD AND SEEN*

Thereafter I was more cautious with my incantation; for I had no wish to be cut off from my body and from the earth in unknown abysses whence I could never return.

H. P. LOVECRAFT, "THE BOOK"

According to the ancient Egyptians, the sleeper dwells in the world of the gods in the next world.[405] In your dreams, you have seen the "other side," and sleep may simply be a "dress rehearsal" for death.

Certain individuals, however, have made more extensive visits.

For example, the ancient Greeks spoke of the "Second-Fated Ones," or people considered dead who had returned. Considered impure, the Second-Fated Ones could not mix with other people or enter a sanctuary until they had undergone a purification ceremony.[330]

To be purified, they were washed, wrapped in swaddling clothes like a newborn baby, and breast-fed. They also had to make a sacrifice to the gods. In effect, they were becoming ritually safe again by symbolically repeating the life cycle.[330]

This section contains a spectrum of accounts of people who died— left the world infested with flesh creatures—and then returned.

The journeys on the other side may seem spectacular, but the Hindus believe that the deceased can travel to the sky, to the earth, to the sun, and to "the whole moving universe," and to "distances beyond the beyond." The deceased can also travel to the past and to the future.[728, 787] In the words of one Hindu sacred text: "The life of the dead wanders as his nature wills."[728, 787]

The journeys described here are *not* dreams. The congenitally blind do not see while dreaming, but, in a trek of the soul, sometimes called a near-death experience, the blind can see.[305]

CROSSING WITHOUT A BRIDGE

Shamanism dominates the religion of hunters and pastoralist peoples.[261] Representing a tradition that may date back to the Ice Age, shamans claim direct contact with the supernatural. (Priests, in contrast, learn their lore from elders and written texts.)[147, 881, 266, 261, 50, 373, 574, 213]

Shamans are special individuals, and they gain their power in various ways.[859] Among the Samoyed people of Siberia, the shaman's vocation passes from father to son.[50] Among the Tlingit Indians in North America, the apprentice spends the night with a shaman's corpse.[266]

Among the Buriat people in Siberia, someone who is struck by lighting and survives becomes a shaman.[265] Among the Jaguar People in Colombia (known as the Kogi), the shaman-to-be spends years in training in what in effect is an ordeal. Taken from his parents at birth, he must not taste meat, behold a woman, or see daylight until he reaches adulthood.[722, 2]

According to the shamans, a bridge once connected the otherworld and the earth, and communication was easy in those times. But now the bridge is broken—the communication is gone—and only the dead or people who are shamans can make the journey.[266, 50]

Professor Eliade (1907–1986), the religious historian, described the experiences of one Eskimo shaman who died—visited the afterworld—and then returned. For shamans, returning from death is not considered unusual. Professor Joseph Campbell (1904–1987) mentioned an Eskimo shaman who allegedly died and resurrected ten times.[139] In one famous account, Richard Johnson, an English traveler, saw a Samoyed shaman die and then reappear alive.[237]

In the Eliade case, the shaman said that after death he traveled for two days. He reached a village, which looked exactly like a village of the living.[266]

There was meat cooking, but he did not eat. According to a widespread tradition, eating would make it difficult—if not impossible—to return to the world of the living.[266, 787, 519]

The shaman continued his journey—he reached the Milky Way—followed it a long time, and then reached his own grave, where he returned to life.[266]

THUNDER CLOUD'S JOURNEY

Another classic description of the post-death adventure is from the Winnebago people of North America. The Winnebago, a Native American people whose ancestral lands are around Green Bay, Wisconsin, have shamans and believe in reincarnation.[441]

Thunder Cloud, a Winnebago shaman, described his own previous deaths.[441] In the first death that he remembered, Thunder Cloud said he was killed in a massacre. He did not realize he was dead until he saw his own mutilated body among a group of corpses. No one buried them, said Thunder Cloud, so they rotted.[441]

Thunder Cloud said he was taken to where the sun set and he lived there with an old couple. This place, called spirit land, is an excellent realm. According to Thunder Cloud, if anyone wants to go somewhere in spirit land, all he must do is to wish himself there.[441]

After spending some time in spirit land, Thunder Cloud decided to go back to the land of the living to avenge his killing. He asked the chief of his village in spirit land, and the chief gave him permission.[441]

So Thunder Cloud entered a womb and was born again. He grew to manhood and avenged his earlier death.[441]

"There I lived until I died of old age," said Thunder Cloud. "All at once my bones became un-jointed, my ribs fell in, and I died a second time. I felt no more pain at death, then, than I had felt the first time."[441, 708]

He was buried in the earth, and "in the grave I rotted." While in the grave, he heard a voice saying, "Come, let us go away."[441]

Thunder Cloud went toward the setting sun. He stayed in a village of the dead for four years. He met the "earth makers," and then he was reborn again.[441]

When Thunder Cloud told his story, he was in his third life.[441]

THE VISION OF ARDA VIRAF

The religion of Zoroaster (or Zarathustra), which still exists, teaches that our ethics in this life determine the nature of our afterlife trek.

It is unclear when Zoroaster existed, but Plutarch (circa 46–120 CE) said that the sage lived "five thousand years before the time of the Trojan War."[694, 912]

The Zoroastrians believe that the soul's journey was experienced firsthand by a man named Arda Viraf. "The Vision of Arda Viraf" gives an account of his visit to other worlds, while he was alive and in a trance.[99, 912]

According to Arda Viraf, if the newly deceased person is good, his soul will spend "three nights . . . seated on the top of the body." Because he was good, he will be filled with joy.

"In the third dawn," he will begin a journey along a fragrant path "into the sweet scent of trees."

There, he will encounter the "graceful form of a damsel," well pleasing and desirable, with prominent breasts and a dazzling face. According to the Avesta, the sacred scriptures of Zoroastrianism, this beautiful virgin is white-armed, noble, and in her fifteenth year.[825, 261] The soul of the good man will ask that damsel thus: "Who art thou? and what person art thou? than whom, in the world of the living, any damsel more elegant, and of more beautiful body than thine, was never seen by me."[99]

But, the mysterious girl will tell the pious man that she is not a woman. She is, in fact, his good thoughts, good words, and good deeds.

Joyous, the good man will then cross a bridge and enter a paradise.

If the newly deceased man is wicked, however, his experiences will be very different.[99]

In those first three nights, he will linger by his corpse, and he will grieve and lament, as "so much mischief and evil" is shown to his soul.[99]

Then, "a stinking cold wind comes to meet him," and he will see a "profligate woman, naked, decayed, gapping, bandy-legged, lean-hipped," a "most hideous, noxious creature," a woman "most filthy and most stinking."[99]

When the wicked soul asks the hag—the disgusting ogress—to identify herself, this woman, who is "uglier, or filthier, or more stinking" than any creature, will reply that she is not a woman at all. In fact, she is his wicked thoughts, his wicked words, and his wicked deeds.[99]

In her words, "I am thy bad actions, O youth of evil thoughts, of evil words, of evil deeds, of evil religion. It is on account of thy will and actions that I am hideous and vile, iniquitous and diseased, rotten and foul-smelling, unfortunate and distressed, as appears to thee."[99]

And, with that, the wicked soul will take four steps and fall into a hell.

SWEDENBORG'S ACCOUNT OF CROSSING

Emanuel Swedenborg, the celebrated Christian seer, also claimed that he saw the other side and directly experienced the afterworlds.

According to Swedenborg, what we call death is "nothing but a crossing from one world to another just like it." Indeed, "because of the resemblance between the spiritual world and the natural world, it is hard for people after death to realize that they are not in the world where they were born, the world they have just left."[840]

The newly dead will also discover that "after death, we enjoy every sense, memory, thought, and affection we had in the world: we leave nothing behind except our earthly body."[840]

In fact, our memories there will be better than our memories here. Everything we have "thought, intended, and done, or seen and heard" during our lives is "inscribed on our inner or spiritual memory."[840] When authors die, for example, they can recall every word in their books exactly.[840]

According to Swedenborg, although a few people enter heaven or hell immediately after death, most go first to an intermediate place called the "World of Spirits."[840] No one stays in the World of Spirits more than thirty years, but there we will see our recently dead family members and friends.[840]

Ultimately, as detailed in chapter IV, our "ruling love" will draw us to a heavenly community or a hellish community.

When we first arrive in the World of Spirits, we have our present faces. Later, however, our faces will change. According to Swedenborg, "the face of our spirit is very different from the face of our body. We get our physical face from our parents and our spiritual faces from our affection, which it images."[840]

Eventually, people with good affections will have "lovely faces" and those engaged in evil affections will have "ugly ones."[840] In effect, what happened to the fictional Dorian Gray, in the classic Oscar Wilde (1854–1900) novella, will happen to evil people.[929]

According to Swedenborg, the face changes because "in the other life no one is allowed to pretend to affections they do not really have," and "we cannot put on a face that is contrary to the love we are engaged in."[840]

In the case of the people in hell, they "appear in the form of their own evil." "In many cases there is no visible face, only something hairy and bony in its place." Their bodies are also misshapen.[840]

When the people in hell look at one another, however, they appear human. "This is a gift of the Lord's mercy, so they do not look as repulsive to each other as they do to angels."[840]

But when a ray of heaven's light shines into hell, the beings there are seen as they are "because in heaven's light everything appears as it really is." That is why they avoid heaven's light and flee from it.[840]

FREEDOM FROM
THE "MASS OF COLD CLAY"

In America, a classic death trek took place in 1889. It was experienced by Dr. A. S. Wiltse, a Kansas physician, who was dead for several hours.[611, 188]

The *St. Louis Medical and Surgical Journal,* November 1899 issue, published a description of Dr. Wiltse's experience.

Apparently killed by typhoid fever, Wiltse had no perceptible pulse for four hours and no detectable breathing for thirty minutes. Physicians in attendance declared him dead.

Wiltse said he felt himself separating from his body "like a soap bubble."[188] He floated up until the separation was complete. He then fell lightly to the floor and resumed the shape of a man.

He said that once he was out of his body, all of the pain and discomfort disappeared.

These are the words of Wiltse:

I seemed to be translucent, of a bluish cast, and perfectly naked. As I turned, my elbow came in contact with the arm of one of two gentlemen standing near the door . . . his arm passed through mine without resistance . . . I . . . saw my own dead body . . . I was surprised at the paleness of the face . . . [I] attempted to gain the attention of the people [at the bedside] with the object of reassuring them of my own immortality, . . . but found they gave me no heed.[611]

Wiltse then described being transported along a beautiful road.

On the road, he found his way barred by a barrier of rocks. He was told that if he crossed the barrier, he could not return to his body.

Then a "small black cloud" touched his face and he was back in his body. That made him feel anguish, astonishment, and disappointment.[611]

Returning to the body after a death experience is commonly described as distasteful: one writer said it was like being drawn into "a mass of cold clay."[306]

EXPERIENCES WITH KETAMINE

Curiously, the drug named ketamine (it is commonly called "Special K"), makes a temporary death trek possible.[306]

First developed in 1962 at the University of Michigan, ketamine is a "dissociation anesthetic" that produces sensory loss without loss of consciousness. It sometimes prompts out-of-body experiences.[306]

Ketamine is openly sold in pharmacies in Mexico, but unauthorized possession of this drug is a felony in the United States.[673]

The effects of the drug are dramatic. Within five minutes, the ego and the anesthetized body are disassociated. Very literally, the person becomes unaware of his own body.[673, 306]

Ketamine experiences resemble classic near-death episodes: the subject experiences a tunnel of light, soaring, a feeling of proximity to a god or gods and dead people, and detachment from the body.[673, 306]

Karl Jansen, a psychiatrist, gave ketamine to volunteers under controlled conditions, and many of his subjects described "becoming a disembodied mind or soul, dying and going to another world." In the words of one individual: "You could fly and actually travel. You are in a place where everybody is who ever died."[854]

What is happening is unclear, but it is possible that ketamine may inhibit brain processes that normally prevent the mind from leaving the body.[305]

THE *BARDO THODOL*

A Traveler's Guide to Other Worlds

In fabled Tibet, the land of Diamond Vehicle Buddhism, the trek of the deceased is described in a religious classic called the *Bardo Thodol* or *Liberation by Hearing in the After-Death Plane*. In the words of British Orientalist Sir John Woodroffe (1865–1936), the book is a "traveler's guide to other worlds."[949]

Written in the eighth century CE by a sage named Padma Sambhava (or Rinpoche),[662, 70] the *Bardo Thodol* was hidden in a cave on the mountain called Gampo Dar. It was found in the fourteenth century by Karma Lingpa (1326–1386).[662, 820] (The *Bardo Thodol* is also known in the West as the *Tibetan Book of the Dead,* a title attributed to it by editor Walter Evans-Wentz.)

The *Bardo Thodol* belongs to a special class of writings called *termas*.[536] Considered treasures, these books are secreted away until the human race is ready for them.[820] Alexandra David-Neel (1868–1969), one of the greatest explorers of the inner and outer worlds of Tibet of the nineteenth and twentieth centuries, wrote that fifty termas have been found.[207] Others still remain hidden.[636]

The *Bardo Thodol*—the most famous of the termas—is NOT based on tradition or faith. Allegedly, it is based on testimony of master adepts who have died and reentered the human womb consciously.[663]

Unlike ordinary people, who wander in the post-death state without a fixed purpose, and whose personalities will disintegrate, these adepts have mastered the art of what Professor Robert Thurman calls "lucid dying."[662] After death their psychic energy remains coherent, and they are reborn with memories in mothers that they have selected.[208] Their experience is NOT a near-death experience. It is a death and conscious rebirth experience.[663, 636]

These great individuals—called *tulkus*—return to help others. Since the fourteenth century, all Tibetan sects have adopted the practice of identifying the rebirths of these great teachers. The most famous is the Dalai Lama, but there are three thousand other lines of incarnation in Tibet.[535]

Unlike some of the other narratives in this chapter, the *Bardo Thodol* is more than a description of the death trek. As part of Diamond Vehicle Buddhism, it belongs to a tradition called the "short path," and by using the methods in the book, one can modify one's post-mortem fate in a positive way. Ordinary beings are controlled by karma, but the Diamond Vehicle Buddhist is not.[208, 70, 636]

Because Diamond Vehicle Buddhism maintains that "all is only mind," "mental acts are the only acts that have any effects at all."[70] Thus, by changing one's conscious thoughts, and by mental purification and concentration, the chain of rebirth and the effects of karma can be broken or abridged.[70] In other words, one may cause oneself to be reborn in the most agreeable conditions possible.[208]

According to Lama Lodru, a Tibetan sage, "These methods are so easy that many people will not believe them, and so deep that most people cannot understand them."[533] The methods must therefore be given only to the properly prepared.[533]

In the First Bardo

According to the *Bardo Thodal,* the death trek may last as long as forty-nine days. The entire process is divided into three periods. Each period is called a *bardo* and each is important.[208]

In the first bardo, the dying person will have these experiences in succession:[536, 70]

1. Mirage vision: vision becomes blurred, and dark images appear. The body becomes weak and powerless, and there is a feeling of falling.

2. Smoke vision: next, the sense of hearing dissolves. Feelings of pleasantness or unpleasantness cease. There is a feeling of being absorbed into smoke.

3. Fireflies: the sense of smell dissolves. Memories of friends and enemies fade away. There is a feeling of being surrounded by sparks or fireflies.

4. Butter-lamp: the sense of taste dissolves and the person can no longer move his body. He no longer thinks of worldly activities. There is the appearance of a dying flame.

Now, breathing ceases. A Western physician would consider the person dead, but in reality the death process continues.

At this point, the "empiric consciousness"—the "consciousness of objects"—is lost.[949] In other words, wherever the person is dying—the hospital room, the battlefield, or the burning automobile—will seem to disappear.

Then the person will experience—from all sides—the "Clear Light of the Void." The subject will experience a colorless light that cannot be described with words. But, it will be as bright as a thousand suns and as loud as a "thousand thunders simultaneously sounding."[663]

During the experience, the deceased will be conscious without any form of body. Even in dreams, we have dream bodies. Here, however, the individual is consciousness alone in the light.[511]

The deceased will have—like a streak of lightning—an intuition of supreme reality. If he can seize the light, he can escape from the round of births and deaths and achieve nirvana.[208]

What is nirvana? For he who embraces the Clear Light, personal consciousness is no more and time is no more.[70] Described in the Buddha's own words, nirvana is "where there is neither death nor birth, there neither is this world nor that, nor in between—it is the ending of sorrow."[663]

Note that nirvana is not technically a place, but "an absence." In the words of one eminent scholar, nirvana is the "absence of suffering in the present and the absence of any possibility of suffering in the future."[535]

Generally, however, the deceased will be dazzled by the Clear Light of the Void and will shrink from it. He will be pulled backward by "false conception," "attachment to individual existence," and the "pleasure of the senses." Or, because of his ignorance, the meaning of the Clear Light will escape him.[208]

If he draws back from the Clear Light of the Void, he will then see a secondary Clear Light, dimmed by illusion.[949]

If the mind does not find release by this point, the first bardo comes to an end. The first bardo may last several days or "for the time it takes to snap a finger."[949]

In the Second Bardo

Next begins the second stage or the second bardo. Trained adepts will pass directly into higher states with no loss of consciousness, but the ordinary person will not. The ordinary person will pass out, as if in a swoon.[70]

After the ordinary person has been dead for a period—about three and a half days for most individuals—he will regain consciousness. Puzzled, he will wonder what happened.[533]

No one will see or hear him. He will see his dead body and will try to enter it, but he cannot. If he is unwise—if he is attached to his physical body—his consciousness may linger near the body for weeks or even years.[533]

(If he is very foolish, when his body is cremated or buried, he may try to enter someone else's body.)[533]

When the dead person's consciousness moves out-of-doors into the sun, he will have no shadow. In a mirror, he will see no reflection. When he walks, he will leave no footprints.[536]

In most cases, he will now realize that he is dead.

Sorrowful and afraid, he will realize that he cannot take anything accumulated over his lifetime: his friends, his family, his wealth, even his own body.[533]

The Mental Body of the Second Bardo

Now he has a "mental body," a kind of a "shining illusionary-body."[663] It seems physical to him, but it is like the body one has in dreams.[637, 949]

By virtue of this mental body, the deceased will have wonderful abilities. He must not indulge in his newly found powers, however. Doing that will only provide more substance to the illusion.[207, 663]

This mental body is indestructible.[637] It feeds on odors and fragrances. (Interestingly, the Greeks believed "In Hades psyches perceive each other by smell alone.")[206] It can go anywhere unimpeded.[637] According to the *Tibetan Book of the Dead,* "It is enough to think of a place to find yourself there immediately, even if it is at the other end of the world."[207, 536]

The deceased must not use his power to wander in places that he has frequented in life or to find people he knows.[207]

Instead, he must place himself in the "empty state of nonattraction and nonaversion." He must place himself in "the state of perfect immobility."[207, 663] The deceased must love nothing and hate nothing. He must embrace nothing and flee from nothing.

Apparent Pilgrimage in the Second Bardo

While still in the second bardo, the deceased will begin *what appears to be* a strange pilgrimage. Most will believe that a real journey is really taking place through lands that really exist and are peopled with real beings.[208]

But the journey is not a journey to places. Instead, the deceased will have visions based on the ideas in his own mind.[207] In the words of the *Bardo Thodol,* "What you see is only a reflection of the contents of your mind sent back to you by the mirror of the void."[207, 363, 663]

Now, when a skeptic reads that the bardo experience is like a dream, he dismisses it as a meaningless hallucination. What he does not understand, however, is that the Tibetans say that the world of the living—the world we are in now—is *also* a dream. Our experiences here are equally illusionary.[70]

In the eloquent words of Alexandra David-Neel, this world is "the dream, rich in suffering, in which we live," and here we are the "prisoners of the creations of our own imaginations."[207]

Because the visions are from our own minds,[663] the visions will be perceived according to the dead person's cultural and religious beliefs.[787] The Tibetans are clear that a Christian will believe that he sees the Christ, a Muslim will believe that he sees an angel or Muhammad, and an atheist, who is a nihilist, will have "visions passing before him as mere forms and colors that may frighten and confuse him."[533, 663]

David-Neel specifically asked a *lama* (a venerated teacher) what happens to a Christian after death, and the lama made this statement:

> They will enter the *bardo,* but what they will see is Issou [Jesus], the angels, demons, paradise, and hell. In their mind they will go back to all the things that they have been taught and in which they believed. . . . The images that populate the dream of this journey and its imaginary vicissitudes will be different from the experiences of a Tibetan, but it will be based on the same reality. . . . Every discarnate soul, whether Tibetan or Christian, will have a tendency to mistake for real events the episodes that supplant one another only in the mind.[207]

Phases of the Death Trek in the Second Bardo

For the first seven days in the second bardo state, the dead person will see visions and colors, and beautiful radiant beings.[208] He will experience a feeling of intense tranquility and perfect knowledge.[637]

Since these first visions are happy and glorious, they will awe the unwise and the uninitiated. In reality, the lovely visions are only projections of his own mind.[663]

Soon afterward, however, the lights will grow fainter and fainter and the visions will become more terrifying.[451]

For the next eight to twelve days, he will see ghastly visions, hideous forms, and repugnant horrors. Fiendish monsters—surrounded by flames—will try to capture the deceased and drink his blood from cups made from human skulls. The deceased will be bewildered and frightened.[208, 637]

Think of the second bardo as initial bliss followed by a relentless plunge into terror. Or, to use the bland words of Walter Evans-Wentz (1878–1965), "The first experiences are happier than the later experiences."[663]

The consciousness of the deceased will try to flee from the horrors, but he cannot. They will follow him wherever he goes because they are inseparable from him. They are from his own mind.[663]

The demonic monsters—called "wrathful deities" by the Tibetans—will have animal heads with human bodies. It is interesting that they resemble the animal-headed gods of ancient Egypt.

The deceased must not surrender to fear. He must resist the delusion. Nothing he sees has any reality.[207] These monsters are projections from his own mind. His thoughts of hate and jealousy—his lusts and his delight in ignorance—the suffering that his malice has caused to others—these things are producing the monsters that he sees.[207]

In the Third Bardo

After many days in the second bardo state, if liberation has not been achieved, the deceased person's past desires and his "thirst for sensations" will become overwhelming. But his lack of "flesh organs" will prevent him from satisfying his cravings.[207]

Now, the desire for embodiment—the desire for rebirth—will become an intolerable torment.[207] The deceased is now moving toward rebirth. He is now in the third bardo.

As he approaches rebirth, he will have four experiences in the third bardo unlike anything in life: a giant rainstorm, a tremendous wind, total darkness, and a noise so loud that it causes terror.[533]

In this bardo, he will also encounter Yama. This experience will be ghastly. In the words of the *Bardo Thodol,*

Tying a rope around your neck, Yama will drag you forward. He will sever [your head] at the neck, extract your heart, pull out your entrails, lick your brains, drink your blood, eat your flesh and suck your bones. Despite this, you will not die. Even as your body is repeatedly cut into pieces, it will be continuously revived. Experiencing being cut into pieces in this way, time after time, will cause enormous suffering.[661]

The deceased must not be afraid, however. He has a mental body that cannot die, and Yama does not exist outside his own bewildering perceptions.[661]

As the time in the third bardo draws to a close, the deceased will be drawn toward certain lights and experiences. These will determine his next birth.

The Realms of Rebirth

The Buddhists say that there are six possible realms of rebirth in "the world of desire": a hellish being, a hungry being, an animal, a human, a demi-god (titan), or a god.[70]

Unlike nirvana, no one stays in any of the six realms forever. One may stay there millions of years, but one will eventually die again and be reborn.[70] In the words of David-Neel: "One dies in hell just as one dies in paradise. One will die in the six classes of being."[207]

If the deceased is going to be born in a hellish realm—a realm produced primarily by hate—he will take pleasure in a smoky light. He will see a black and red house. He will hear beautiful music that he can barely resist.[533, 661]

He must not go there. The Buddhist hell is temporary, but it can last millions of years.[547, 176]

If he is going to be born in the hungry ghost realm (the "Pretan" realm)—a realm produced by greed—he will be attracted to a yellow light and he will feel that he is entering a heap of burnt wood.[533, 662]

He must not go there. Although Pretans are sometimes called "hungry ghosts," they are not ghosts. They are living beings caught in a realm of extreme frustration—hunger, thirst, and craving torment them—but their food is hard to gather, difficult to swallow, and burns when they eat.[662]

If he is going to be reborn as an animal—a subhuman being—he will be drawn to a green light and he will experience passing into a cave.[533, 661]

He must not go there. The animal realm is a product of ignorance, folly, and stupidity, and animals suffer from their lack of intelligence and their limited ability to communicate.[662]

If he is going to be born as a human, he will be drawn to a blue light and he will see erotic images of humans copulating. If he is attracted to the woman and is repulsed by the man, he will be born a human male. If he is attracted to the man and has an aversion to the woman, he will be born a human female.[662, 533]

The moment that he has these feelings about the copulating humans, he will enter the woman's womb. The copulating couple will become his human parents.[662, 533]

If the deceased can be born as a human, he should. Like all Eastern religions, Buddhists regard being human as a precious treasure: it is achieved only after hundreds of thousands or millions of lifetimes and is a magnificent achievement.[662, 636] (Likewise, one Hindu sage said it requires eight million lives to achieve the human state.)[955]

According to Buddhism, only a human can attain nirvana. (Technically, a non-human can attain deliverance, but it is extremely difficult.)[665] Hellish beings and hungry ghosts are too tormented to find enlightenment. Animals are too ignorant and stupid. Gods and demigods—the beings above humans—are too immersed in power, pleasure, and bliss.[535]

If he is to be reborn as a jealous god (a titan or demi-god), he will be attracted to a red light. He will feel that he is entering a lovely garden or a place of great natural beauty.[533, 661]

If the deceased enters the realm of the *asuras* (titans or anti-gods), he will live in a heaven-like realm near the gods, and he will have risen to a state above human level.[662]

The titans, however, love power. Jealousy drives them. They enjoy combat, and they constantly try to seize the heaven realms from the gods.[662] Constant fighting and killing and dying habituate them to rage, and they tend to fall down eventually to hells.[662]

If the deceased is to be reborn as a god (*deva*), he will be attracted to a dull white light (the color of moonlight) and he will have the feeling that he is entering a great heavenly palace.[533]

Beings in the god realm have ascended from the human state through generosity, sensitivity, and tolerance. According to Lama Lodru, to be born as a god is "a result of great merit, but not yet perfect merit."[533]

The gods, as great beings, have comforts, pleasure, power, and long lifetimes. Lower realms seem far away to them.[662, 661] But gods have so much comfort and power that they are dominated by pride and tend to fall back to the human level after millions of years.[662]

In the words of Marco Pallis (1895–1989), an authority on Tibet:

> The gods here referred to are not immortal and self-sufficient dei-ties, but simply beings of an order higher than ours, possessed of wider powers than man's such as longevity, unfading beauty, and freedom from pain, except at last when they are about to cease from being gods, and turn into something lower, for then their charms begin to wither, and their fragrance turns to stench so foul that their goddess-wives flee from their presence.[665]

In Tibet they do not worship these gods because these beings are on the wheel of rebirth. To Tibetans, true divinities are those in Buddhahood.[665]

Beyond Bardo: Becoming Free of Illusion

To summarize the essential idea of the *Bardo Thodol,* Diamond Vehicle Buddhism teaches that *illusions persist even after death.* To be free to enjoy nirvana, we must free ourselves from all illusion.

If we can recognize the illusions for what they are, we are liberated.

Or, to use the words of Sir John Woodroffe, "Man is in fact liberated, but does not know it. When he realizes it, he is freed."[949]

Clearly, Diamond Vehicle Buddhism views death as a time of great opportunity and great danger.[535]

To make wise choices in the bardo states, we must train now. As Lama Lodru says in *Bardo Teachings,* if we encounter a person that we have never met before, we will not recognize him. Likewise, without training we will not recognize what we are experiencing in the bardo states.[533]

Interestingly, Professor Robert Thurman, an expert on Tibetan Buddhism, suggests that while alive—instead of "sleeping mindlessly like an animal"[662]—we should practice the art of lucid dreaming. A lucid dream, of course, is dreaming while being aware that we are dreaming.[662]

According to Professor Thurman, if we can dream lucidly—if we can train ourselves to become self-aware in dreams—it will be easier to remain lucid in the dreams that are the bardo states.[662]

What is the best way to train ourselves to dream lucidly?

Theosophist Oliver Fox (1885–1949), the pseudonym of Hugh Calloway, described one technique. Fox claimed that he was able to become aware during a dream by deliberately taking note of any oddity or incongruity in the dream setting. Once he was aware of the oddity, Fox claimed he was able to move about independently in the dream with full conscious awareness.[310, 879, 17]

VI
Afterlife
How to Enter Other Worlds

Like corn, a man ripens and falls to the ground; like corn,
he springs up again in his season.

KATHA UPANISHAD

Nothing dies forever.

ODIN BROTHERHOOD

Make death die.

VALENTINUS (CIRCA 100–160)

Death is really a return to the beginning.

P. D. OUSPENSKY, *A NEW MODEL OF THE UNIVERSE*

You sleep that you may wake; you die that you may live.

EGYPTIAN PYRAMID TEXTS

Not all of me shall die.

HORACE (65–8 BCE)

It is by no means clear that the universe is just, that there is any sense in which the universe must be just, or indeed that it would necessarily be any more just if there were an afterlife.

PROFESSOR CARL B. BECKER,
*BREAKING THE CIRCLE: DEATH AND
THE AFTERLIFE IN BUDDHISM*

Jesus answered him, "I tell you the truth, today you will be with me in paradise."

LUKE 23:43

And the serpent said to the woman, "Ye shall not surely die: For God doth know that in the day ye eat thereof, then your eyes shall be opened, and ye shall be as gods, knowing good and evil."

GENESIS 3:4-5

He who sees this, who knows this, who understands this, who desires the soul, who plays with the soul, who makes love with the soul, who attains voluptuousness with the soul, becomes his own master and wanders at will through the worlds. But they who know otherwise are dependent. They dwell in perishable worlds and cannot wander at their will.

CHANDOGYA UPANISHAD

That the saints may enjoy their beatitude and the Grace of God more abundantly, they are permitted to see the punishment of the damned in hell.

ST. THOMAS AQUINAS

Three will not see the face of judgment in Gehenna: Those
who suffer from grinding poverty, abdominal diseases, and
creditors. Some add to this: anyone married to a nasty
wife.

AKIVA BEN JOSEPH
(CIRCA 40–CIRCA 137 CE)

This section contains information—facts that are "skeleton keys"—to open the other worlds.

When different traditions give different instructions, do not despair. According to Eastern sages, the same truth looks different from several viewpoints.[665]

Since their ways of life are so varied, it is not surprising that the religion of the hunter does not resemble the religion of the farmer, or the religion of the factory worker. Man the hunter lives by killing; man the farmer lives by growing; man the factory worker lives by fashioning "commodities." Since their lives are so different, their religious conceptions are also different.

In particular, as Joseph Campbell points out in *The Masks of God,* man the factory worker has replaced the shamans of the hunter and the priests of the farmer with "the magic of the laboratory." With scientists "flying rocket ships where gods once sat," man the factory worker has lost faith in the gods and bows down to technology.[139]

In this chapter, I have tried to be representative, but the list of "skeleton keys" is not complete. Buddhism alone speaks of the 84,000 paths of enlightenment.[834]

THE POWER OF SHIVA

Shiva's abode and paradise is Kailasa, also called Swastika Mountain.[481] It is open to all who worship Shiva, regardless of caste or gender.[487]

Although the Hindus have many afterworlds, Swastika Mountain is especially interesting because it is located on earth. The only mountain on the planet not climbed by man, no one has ever been allowed on the summit because the Hindus believe that Shiva and his paradise are there.[605, 296, 548, 481, 592]

In *Skanda Purana,* a wicked thief is killed by the king's men. A dog comes to eat the thief, but accidently, and without thought, the dog's nails make the mark of Shiva's trident on the man's forehead. As a result, Shiva's messengers take the thief to Shiva's paradise.[238]

Such is the power of Shiva.

Die in Benares, the Holy City of Shiva

The ancient city of Benares, also known as Varanasi or Kashi, is a city situated on the banks of the Ganges River in the Indian state of Uttar Pradesh.[826] A "place never deserted by god," Benares is the most famous of the holy cities of India.[487, 481, 202] It is said that those whose eyes are purified can still see the fire lingam of Shiva there. The fire lingam, very literally, is the phallus of the god.[826]

Many Hindus go to the city to die, and funeral pyres burn there day and night. According to legend, the fire used to cremate the dead has never been rekindled since it was taken from the first fire on earth.[826]

Hindus believe that anyone who dies in Benares need not fear punishment or rebirth.[487] In Benares, they can achieve liberation.[105] These are the words of Shiva in the *Matsya Purana*:

> Varanasi is always my most secret place; the cause of liberation for all creatures. All sins which a man may have accumulated in thousands of previous lives disappear as soon as he enters the "place never deserted by god." Brahmins, Ksatriyas, Vaisyas, and Sudras, people of mixed castes, worms, *mlecchas* [barbarians, or people without the Vedas[64]], and other casteless people, insects, ants, birds, all mortal beings find bliss in my auspicious city.[564]

Visit Shiva's Temple at Somnathpur

Visit Shiva's temple at Somnathpur in India and all of your sins are forgiven.[826, 932, 238]

Kill or Cut Out the Tongue of Someone Who Reviles Shiva

The *Linga Purana,* a Hindu text, promises Shiva's heaven to anyone who kills or tears out the tongue of someone who reviles the god Shiva.[487]

PROCREATE A SON BEFORE YOU DIE

In many traditions, having a son is somehow essential to the well-being of a man and his deceased ancestors.[218]

According to the Konde people in Africa, a man will return as a frog if his family line ends with him.[9]

According to the *Epic of Gilgamesh* from Mesopotamia, in the otherworld a man with seven sons sits on a throne with the gods, but a man with no sons eats bread that resembles bricks.[277]

According to the *Aitareya Brahmana,* a Hindu text, "By means of a son have fathers always crossed over the deep darkness, since he was born as their self from their self."[14, 120]

And Alain Daniélou (1907–1994), the French historian, Indologist, and a Western convert to Shaivite Hinduism (the type of Hinduism especially devoted to the god Shiva), wrote these words: "For the person who has no descendants, who breaks the lineage of his ancestors, the 'I' disappears at death, although it may sometimes attach itself for a time to certain subtle elements, producing phantoms."[204]

BE REBORN IN THE WOMB OF YOUR LOVER

Abhayadera Suri, an eleventh-century Jain of the "white-clad" sect, claimed that a man who died in the act of sexual intercourse will be reborn in the womb of his lover.[249, 120]

COME BACK AS A LION

Some Africans believe that we can come back as an animal, but Zulus say only chiefs come back as lions.[9, 255]

COME BACK FROM YOUR BONES

As Professor Mircea Eliade (1907–1986) pointed out, a characteristic belief of hunting cultures is that living things can be reborn from their skeletons.[261, 266] Thus, when hunters kill game, they do not break the bones because they expect the resurrection of the dead individual from the bones (especially the skull and long bones).[266, 50, 261, 139, 472, 830]

The Eskimo, for example, leave the skull of a bear they have killed face down at the place where the bear was slain. This, they believe, allows it to be reborn.[147]

For the same reason, Indians from the Pacific Northwest region of America put salmon bones back in water.[441]

For people in planting cultures, the dead body, including the bones, disintegrate and germinate into something else. For the hunter, in contrast, one part of the dead body, the bone, becomes the "undestroyed base" from which the same individual is "magically reconstructed."[139]

HAVE YOUR BONES PLACED
IN THE GANGES RIVER

Although mentioned only twice in the Hindu Vedas,[932] the most sacred river in India is the Ganges.

Although the Hindus believe that all moving or falling water can purify,[481] the waters of the Ganges are believed to have special powers. To die while immersed in the Ganges results in *moksa,* or final liberation from the wheel of rebirth.[481] Moreover, simply being touched by a breeze containing a drop of Ganges water erases all sins accumulated over all lifetimes.[481]

The Hindus also say that as long as the bones of a person (even a fraction of a bone) are lying in the Ganges River, or even touching Ganges water, they can remain in a heavenly realm.[487]

Many Hindus say that if anyone should manage to pour Ganges water on the Kaaba, the focus of Muslim devotion in Mecca, it would cause the beginning of the end for Islam. Because the Kaaba is well protected, such an act has never occurred.[488]

DIE FROM OLD AGE

The tribes of north Nigeria believe that a person who dies of old age has a vigorous soul (that is how he reached old age), and when he goes to the next world, he has power.[313]

To extend life—and to reach old age—Marsilio Ficino (1433–1499), a Renaissance writer, described a rather curious rejuvenation procedure:

> Therefore choose a young girl who is healthy, beautiful, cheerful, and temperate, and when you are hungry and the moon is waxing, place your mouth at her breasts and draw their milk, and then immediately eat a bit of fennel powder thoroughly mixed with sugar syrup.[144]

GRADUALLY BECOME A SPIRIT

The Houailou people, a Melanesian group found in New Caledonia in the Pacific Ocean, see life as a process of "becoming spirit." As we grow older, we shed humanness and we take on the character of spirits.[837]

KNOW THE SECRET PASSWORDS

Orpheus, son of the king of Thrace and the muse named Calliope,[340] was a musician, mystic, and poet. According to the ancient Greeks, Orpheus lived a generation before the Trojan War.[130]

So beautiful was his music—when hearing it, even brute animals lost their wildness—that the lyre of Orpheus was ultimately transformed into the constellation Lyra.[964, 140, 340]

Orpheus married a beautiful nymph named Eurydice. Tragically, when a shepherd tried to rape her, she fled, stepped on a serpent, and died from the venom. A poem by Virgil (70–19 BCE) contains a complete account of Orpheus and Eurydice.[897]

Orpheus, like the heroes Heracles and Theseus, actually visited the land of the dead while still living.[444] Entering a cave at Taenarum (Cape Tenaron in Greece), Orpheus tried to bring Eurydice back to our world.[9]

By charming all with his music, Orpheus almost succeeded, but ultimately he failed. Eurydice remained in the otherworld.[9]

Filled with grief, Orpheus never looked at another woman. Instead, he surrounded himself with juvenile males and invented pederasty, the sexual intercourse between an adult man and a boy.[354, 680] (This became common in ancient Greece, and Plato, in his *Symposium,* curiously said that pederasty, nude sports, and philosophy were the three things that exalted the Greeks above the barbarians.)[692]

The pederasty of Orpheus enraged many of the women of Thrace— Orpheus was the most desirable of men—so the women violently dismembered him.[354, 680]

Around this enigmatic figure, the mystery cult of Orpheus developed.[340] Allegedly, Orpheus discovered secrets about the afterlife when he went to the underworld to find Eurydice, and these secrets were imparted to initiates in a private brotherhood.[433, 444, 261]

According to the Orphic mysteries, rebirth is inevitable, but also undesirable. The sage must escape from this rebirth.[340]

When a non-initiate dies, he goes to Hades. Eventually, his soul will wither and die there, but his divine spark will be reincarnated into another body and soul.[340]

The Orphic initiate, however, escapes this circle of grief and goes to a glorious destiny among the gods. To reach that destiny after death, his cremated remains are buried with special instructions. These instructions contain specific information on what he should say and do when he awakens after death.[340, 443]

Interpreting the Secret Instructions

The Orphic secrets were lost for centuries, but archaeologists digging in the ruins of the ancient city of Hipponion (a Greek settlement in the modern Italian province of Calabria) discovered a stone chest. Inside the chest, they found a small piece of gold foil covered with a Greek text.

Based on the style, the text was dated to approximately 400 BCE.[75, 361]

They had discovered an Orphic golden plate. Sixteen such texts have now been found in tombs throughout the Mediterranean world.[443, 75]

In the instructions on the golden plates, "Hades" refers to the lord of the dead, the black-haired brother of Zeus. He has a helmet of invisibility; thus, no one sees the approach of death.[354, 330]

"The spring" refers to the Fountain of Forgetfulness (Lethe or Oblivion). Located to the left, drinking this water obliterates all memory.

"The lake" refers to the Pool of Memory (Mnemosyne). The water from this pool allows the adept to keep his memory and his personality in the next world.[891]

The instructions and passwords are given as follows:

You will find to the left of the House of Hades a spring. By the side
    of the spring is a white cypress. Do NOT approach this spring.
You will also find the Pool of Memory. There is cold water in the
    pool, and there are guardians standing before it.
Say to the guardians these secret passwords:

> *I am a child of Earth and starry Heaven;*
> *but my race is of Heaven alone.*
> *This you know yourselves.*
> *But I am parched with thirst and I perish.*
> *Give me quickly the cold water*
> *flowing forth from the Pool of Memory.*

The guardians, having heard the special words, will give you water
    to drink from the holy pool, and "thereafter you will have
    lordship among the other heroes."[361, 104, 75, 569]

BELONG TO THE NOBLE CLASS

The Tonga Islands in the Pacific, inhabited by a Polynesian people, developed what might be the most "aggressively unequal" society in history.[110] In traditional Tonga, the nobles could beat and kill the commoners and sexually enjoy all lower-class women at will.[110]

Not unexpectedly, in the Tongan religion the souls of the nobles survive death, and go to Pulotu, a paradise "from which the gods came and to which the souls of deceased chiefs go."[837, 336, 558, 900, 312]

Commoners, however, have no souls. With death, they perish with their bodies.[312] In other words, they simply decompose.[837, 336, 548, 900, 312]

Sir James Frazer (1854–1941) said that he knew of no other culture with such a belief.[313]

LIVE 8,400,000 AEONS AND THEN START AGAIN

Makkhali Gosala (born 484 BCE) was an ascetic teacher of ancient India. The founder of the Ajivika movement, he may have been a contemporary of Siddhartha Gautama, the founder of Buddhism, and of Mahavira, the twenty-fourth pathfinder of Jainism.[204, 62]

Gosala taught that all souls must run through a fixed number of inevitable births during the normal course of their evolution. These births occur over 8,400,000 aeons (*mahakalpas*).[62, 261]

This natural biological activity, said Professor Heinrich Robert Zimmer, "cannot be hurried by means of virtue and asceticism, or delayed because of vice; for the process takes place in its own good time."[963]

According to Gosala, we begin as a living atom. We have only the sense of touch. As we progress, we gain more senses and higher mental faculties and we pass through various types of vegetable life, lower and higher animals, and then human level, and even seven lives as gods.[62, 200]

After all of these existences, release simply happens. The process is automatic and requires no effort from us.[261, 62, 200]

And then, in endless time, the process repeats, from the beginning.[279]

WILLFULLY STARVE YOURSELF

Not only did the great philosopher Pythagoras (570–495 BCE) starve himself to death,[139] but a "death fast" is found in several traditions.

The Cathars, members of a religion that advocated poverty and virginity, as well as nonviolence and truthfulness, practiced Endura or self-starvation. Cathars performed the death fast only after undergoing a mystical initiation ceremony called the Consolation, which made them "perfected ones." The Consolation removed all sins, but it could be performed only once in a lifetime. By linking the two ceremonies—the Consolation and Endura—a Cathar could die in a pure spiritual state.[51, 139]

In Jainism, known for its puritan masochism, the most holy death is self-starvation.[534] As mentioned in Jain scripture, the Jains believe that one may rid oneself of all karmic influences by mortifying the flesh, stopping all physical and mental activities, and starving to death.[963]

Nine of the twelve disciples of Mahavira (dates unknown, but perhaps 540–468 BCE) voluntarily chose this death, and devoted Jains continue the practice today.[822]

Called the "religious death," the Jain death fast is done by monks, nuns, and laypeople.[534] (Even when he is not engaging in a death fast, a Jain monk ordinarily eats only two meatless meals each day, with thirty-two mouthfuls of food at each meal.)[249] The religious death is not considered suicide because it is done without passion and without "poison or weapons."[249, 503]

One must practice the death fast only if one's motives are pure. Performed out of compassion, the Jain embraces this "holy, self-chosen death" in the spirit of peace. By not eating, he is saving other living things by not consuming them.[120, 534, 249, 822]

OPEN YOUR MIND

The Jains speak of *jnanavarniya*—or knowledge-obstructing karma. This kind of karma is generated by the refusal to learn, by the closing of the mind, by the spreading of false or one-sided information, by ridiculing those who pursue knowledge, and by advocating fanatical and prejudiced opinions.[715]

Study all knowledge—reflect on all ideas—and you will rise to higher levels in the process of rebirth. On the other hand, if you denounce books you have never read, condemn people you have never known, and reject ideas you could never understand, you will regress in the process of rebirth.

HANG YOURSELF

Laurence Shirley, the fourth Earl Ferrers, was the last member of the House of Lords hanged in England. Executed for murder in 1760, the hangman reputedly used a rope of silk.[469]

Oddly, according to the Maya, if Laurence Shirley had hanged *himself,* he would now be in paradise. He would be sharing the company of Gerard de Nerval (1808–1855), the French poet who hanged himself in 1855.[817]

According to Diego de Landa (1524–1579), the Maya believe that suicide by hanging is an honorable way to die.[221] Ixtab, or "Rope Woman," is the Mayan goddess of suicide, and she accompanies such suicides to a paradise, a place free from all want.[860, 221]

(In contrast, Jewish law, as described in Deuteronomy 21:23, says that a hanged man is cursed by god. See also Galatians 3:13 in the Christian Bible.)

DIE A WARRIOR'S DEATH

Odin, a warrior deity, lives in Asgard, the stronghold of the Norse gods, where he presides over fabled Valhalla, the hall of the heroic slain. Thatched with golden shields, accessed by hundreds of doors, Valhalla is the most magnificent of all structures.[697, 830]

Unlike the Christian heaven, which is a gift for the life lived by the faithful (who kneel, believe, and obey),[592] Odin's Valhalla is earned by the *mode* of death. Specifically, Odin's Valhalla is open to intrepid warriors who die heroic deaths.[790, 519, 592]

In peaceful urban cultures, a bloody death is viewed as undesirable; city dwellers want a quiet death, a "straw death"—a death in bed from old age or sickness—where the soul exits peacefully through the mouth of the dying man.[592]

But in a violent death, the treasured death of warriors, the soul exits quickly and cleanly through the gaping wound. About such deaths, the Greek Heraclitus (circa 535–circa 475 BCE) said, "Souls slain in war are purer than those that perish with disease. They arise into wakefulness."[206]

Warlike cultures maintain that, in addition to being purer, the war dead reach the next world in a more vigorous form. Writing about the warlike people of Mangaia (the second largest of the Cook Islands in the Pacific Ocean), one author noted that the people think "that the spirits of those who die a natural death are extremely feeble and weak, as their bodies were at dissolution; whereas the spirits of those who are slain in battle are strong and vigorous, their bodies not having been reduced by disease."[335, 308]

And, since many traditions teach that the soul has the age and appearance of the dead person at the time of death, young men who die here are young men over there. This belief inspired Yukio Mishima (1925–1970), a warrior in the Japanese Bushido tradition, and he committed suicide by *seppuku* in 1970 while still relatively young. According to Mishima, a "powerful, tragic frame and sculptured muscles" are "indispensable in a romantically noble death."[823, 619]

Since the medieval Norse people were warriors, their ideal death was a "blood work." The mighty Ragnar Lodbrok, imprisoned by his enemies in a pit filled with squirming snakes, was violently killed by the reptiles. According to Norse texts, Ragnar Lodbrok spoke these final words:

> I'll drink beer with the gods;
> hope of life is lost now,
> laughing shall I die![761]

Like any warrior culture, however, the Northmen knew that sometimes brave men did *not* fall on the field of battle. Midgard, the world of men, is a place of misadventure and plague, so Odin provided a master key to Valhalla to his brave acolytes. A special rite, called "marking with the spear," is described in the *Ynglinga Saga,* and the text notes that both

Odin himself and the god Njord underwent the procedure.[519, 831, 876] In the words of H. M. Chadwick, the author of *The Cult of Othin,* "the rite was clearly regarded by the writer of *Ynglinga Saga* as a substitution for death in battle."[158, 380, 831]

Among modern Odinist pagans, a version of the Odin rite lives on among a group called the Odin Brotherhood. The ritual, which leads to Valhalla, is conducted by initiates who join the group. Involving solitude, a diet of bread and ice, a white death shroud, wood from a lightning-struck tree, a fire, and three cuts to the flesh, the procedure is conducted once per life, and only at the solstices, a threshold time when supernatural forces seep into this world.[592, 946]

Moreover, when initiated members of the Odin Brotherhood do approach death, they make a wound on the body, so that the soul may escape cleanly and strongly. They are buried standing up—like Hrap in the saga story—because fierce warriors stand erect, even in death.[515, 519, 592]

Since Odin promised that in the next world a man would "enjoy whatever he himself had buried in the earth,"[831] before death the resourceful Odinist will bury possessions and treasures. These possessions are first broken or burned, because—just as killing a man dispatches him to the next world—breaking or burning objects conveys them to the other side.[592]

DIE GIVING BIRTH

In many cultures, death during childbirth is viewed as the female equivalent of war. At the time I am writing this, childbirth kills 1,400 women on earth each day.[424] On average, that exceeds the number of men killed daily in war.[592]

Interestingly, in the *Grimnismal,* one of the Norse *Eddaic Verses,* the lovely Freyja, a goddess, takes half of the heroic dead, and this is probably a reference to women who die giving birth.[697, 272, 593, 529]

Another warrior culture, the Aztecs, promised a glorious existence with the sun god for women who died giving birth.[523]

BE REBORN THROUGH FEAR

Curiously, Plato (429–347 BCE), the misogynistic Greek philosopher, writes in *Timaeus* that cowardly males are reincarnated as women.[693, 961]

In Hinduism, however, the *Bhagavata Purana* says that all men in this world were women in their previous births, and vice versa, and that each died thinking about the opposite gender.

THE POWER OF WILL

In *Ligeia,* the haunting Edgar Allan Poe (1809–1849) tale about a slender beauty with long black hair, Poe repeats the powerful words of Joseph Glanvill (1636–1680): "Man doth not yield himself . . . unto death utterly, save only through the weakness of his feeble will."

The tale is fiction, but the philosopher Arthur Schopenhauer (1788–1860) argues in *The World as Will and Representation,* that the will to live does not die, but manifests itself anew in new individuals. To gain deliverance from rebirth (if nonexistence can be called deliverance), you must deny the will to live.

Schopenhauer called his idea *palingenesis,* from the Greek words meaning "again" and "birth." Very literally, if your will to live is strong, you will come back.[770]

ACQUIRE FAME

Ovid (43 BCE–17/18 CE), the great Roman writer, closed his *Metamorphoses* with this line: "I shall live for all eternity, immortalized by fame."[658]

Humbert Humbert, the fictional character in Vladimir Nabokov's novel *Lolita,* makes this celebrated statement: "This is the only immortality you and I may share, my Lolita."[613]

Erostratus, who set fire to the Temple of Artemis in Ephesus (fourth century before the current era), committed the crime to make his name famous.[527]

Fame is difficult to achieve—of the billions who have died since the last Ice Age, only a small number are remembered today[209]—but can fame conquer death?

In many traditions, fame can indeed preserve us beyond the grave.

According to archaic Greek paganism, the dead live *only* as long as the living remember and honor them.[738]

According to Egyptian paganism, if a person's name no longer exists, the person no longer exists,[114] but "to say the name of the deceased is to make him live again."[115]

In Egyptian paganism, the *ren,* or the name, is one of a person's most important attributes, and "any person who effected the blotting out of a man's name was thought to have destroyed him also."[127] Thus, there is some evidence that ancient Egyptian courts "obliterated the names of the guilty" when they were executed. By killing the body and erasing the name, the person ceased to exist at all levels.[250]

In Melanesia, an area of the Pacific, we find similar ideas, and "the existence of the dead seems to be dependent on the memory of the living; when they are forgotten they cease to exist."[312]

In the case of one Melanesian people, the Koita, tillers of the soil in New Guinea, all the dead—good and bad, strong and weak, young and old—go to an afterworld, but they will not abide there forever. They will endure a long time, but, eventually, they will grow weaker and die a second death, never to be reborn. According to Sir James Frazer, "they survive only so long as their names and their memories survive among the living. When these are utterly forgotten, the poor ghosts cease to exist."[312]

And Frazer also made this observation about the Koita: "Their names are in a sense their souls, so that oblivion of the name involves extinction of the soul."[312]

TRAVEL FOREVER WITH AN EGYPTIAN GOD

The Egyptian concept of the afterlife is quite fascinating. In effect, the afterlife is a journey without end.[261]

An important aspect of the Egyptian afterlife is to return to the land of the living—our world—at dawn. In Egyptian religion, the only life is in this world. If the dead live, it is only because they participate in their way in the life of the living.[250]

According to the Egyptian religion, the sun god is born every morning in the womb of the sky goddess, travels across the sky in a boat, along the "celestial" Nile, and every evening he dies in the west, in the arms of his mother.[610, 926]

Every night, in his boat, the dead sun god Ra travels in the underworld, facing perils and obstacles. This underworld is called Duat. Its obstacles include Apophis, a fearsome serpent.[610]

If he successfully survives these perils, the sun god is reborn again in the morning.[610] The sun god's journey in the underworld is described in the *Book of Am-Duat (Of That which Is in the Underworld),* and it is also described in *The Book of Gates.*[926]

According to the Egyptians, the sun god moves from place to place endlessly. He spends half the time journeying through the netherworld realms of darkness and danger, and the other half journeying through the celestial realms of light and abundance.[787]

In the company of the sun god, the souls of the dead make the same journey every night. At first, only the pharaoh traveled with the dead sun god. Later, nobles also made the journey. Still later, other souls went as well.[610]

At sunrise, the dead go to their own homes *here.* At sunset, they gather at Abydos, in Egypt, to repeat the journey for eternity.[610]

In the cryptic words of the *Book of the Dead,* the deceased "shall go forth by day from the otherworld, and he shall enter after he has come out."[610, 126]

To Endure, Know the Magic Spells

To survive this endless journey, the deceased needs magical knowledge.

In the Egyptian religion, immortality is a scholarly path. He who knows the spells and the magical names will endure.[471]

With magic, the dead person has power: he can neutralize monsters in the next world, he can open sealed gates that impede his way, and he can become a worthy companion of the gods and goddesses.[114, 471]

In the afterworld, we can be killed a second time, but magic can protect us. According to Egyptian scholar Alfred Wiedemann (1856–1936), "Both in this world and the next, the best, and indeed the only helpful precautionary measure against any threatened danger was the knowledge of the appropriate spell."[926]

Finding the Magical Knowledge

When we think of Egypt, we think of the great pyramid of Khufu. Built from more than two million limestone blocks, each averaging two and a half tons, the amazing structure is 480 feet tall and its base covers thirteen acres.[114]

The pyramid structure is inherently strong, and workmen using tools would need as much effort to deconstruct it as was needed to build it. As a result, the great pyramid will not only outlast the human race, but it may be the only product of human hands that is nearly eternal.

Another pharaoh, the man named Unas, the last king of Egypt's fifth dynasty, built a sixty-two-foot pyramid that contains beautiful hieroglyphs inside. Those hieroglyphs—all magical in nature—are the *Pyramid Texts,* the oldest known writing about the Egyptian afterlife.[116]

Originally, these spells were for royalty only, but ultimately this knowledge spread. Scholars suggest that the chaos following the collapse of the Old Kingdom let commoners break into the pyramids and learn the spells.[116]

By the so-called Middle Kingdom, non-royals were inscribing similar texts on the sides of their coffins to insure immortality. These texts are known as the *Coffin Texts.*[116]

By the so-called New Kingdom, the spells became so numerous that they were eventually written on papyrus, leather, or linen and placed between the legs of the mummy. Known as *The Going Forth by Day,* modern people refer to this volume of spells as the *Book of the Dead.*[116, 471, 126]

A few thousand copies of the *Book of the Dead* survive to this day. The British Museum has twenty-four copies and the Louvre has more than seventy.[471]

All the necessary magic is contained in each of these three texts: In life, study the *Pyramid Texts,* the *Coffin Texts,* or the *Book of the Dead.* In death, arrange to have any one of these texts placed in your tomb. Their spells will protect you in the next world and empower you to travel forever with the sun god.[114, 127, 471]

The spells should not be translated. Iamblichus (circa 245–circa 325 CE) states, in *Theurgia; Or, The Egyptian Mysteries,* that ancient Egyptian exceeds even the classical Greek language in potency. Egyptian spells have been empowered by thousands of years of repetition.[422]

BECOME A MUMMY

Fascinated by Egypt, in 1852, Alexander, the tenth duke of Hamilton, arranged to be mummified in the Egyptian fashion. He was buried on his estate with full Egyptian magical rites, with Thomas Pettigrew, the archaeologist, acting as the priest.[114, 20]

In effect, the duke joined the half a billion mummies left by the ancient Egyptians.[931] Some of these mummies belonged to the gods themselves. Thebes, the great ceremonial center in Egypt, had the tombs of eight gods.[405]

The mummification process could be quite elaborate—the mummy of Ramses II is so well preserved that we can still see his blackheads[479]— but there were also simpler and cheaper procedures for the poor. In one simple method, cedar oil was injected into the anus, the anus was sealed with linen and mud, and the body was put in natron, a sacred Nile salt. After a time, the liquefied stomach, liver, and intestines were poured out of the anus, and the corpse was then bandaged.[20]

Why did the Egyptians embalm the dead?

Clearly, the mummy was "filled with magic,"[41] and Florence Farr, in her *Egyptian Magic,* argues that the purpose of mummification is to *prevent* reincarnation, or the return of the deceased as *someone else.*

By preserving the body as a kind of magical talisman, the mummy preserves the personality and allows the deceased to keep his connection with the living.[290, 365]

Margaret Murray, the noted Egyptologist, correctly pointed out that Egyptologists mistakenly tend to ignore the Egyptian belief in reincarnation.[610] Indeed, Diodorus Siculus (flourished 30 BCE) said that Pythagoras learned about reincarnation from Egypt.[406, 789] These are the words of Herodotus (circa 484–425 BCE), the ancient historian:

> The Egyptians were the first who asserted that the soul of man is immortal, and that when the body perishes it enters into some other animal, constantly springing into existence; and that when it has passed through the different kinds of terrestrial, marine and aerial beings, it again enters into the body of a man that is born; and that this revolution is made in three thousand years.[389]

Many cultures cremate the powerful dead to prevent their return.[519, 738] It would make sense that the Egyptians would preserve bodies—mummify them—to keep the dead close by and unchanged.

Of course, if you are mummified, as the Duke of Hamilton was, do not forget to have a magical text, such as *The Going Forth by Day*, placed in your tomb.

Mummification may preserve your personality, but you will need magic in the next world to survive its perils. Even mummified gods—such as the eight at Thebes—need magic to survive.

POSE FOR A SCULPTURE OR PAINTING

According to one magical principle, the principle of "sympathetic" or "imitative" magic, if two things resemble one another in form, there is a connection. This is seen in the voodoo doll. Any action on the doll—such as an action to preserve it—will be an action on the original.[314, 213]

Steeped in magic, Egyptian paganism emphasized the importance of crafting statues and paintings of the deceased. As long as the images exist, according to the magical lore, so did the person.

Thus, in ancient Egyptian, the word for *sculptor* means literally "He who keeps alive."[222]

BECOME A VOODOO GOD
OR GODDESS

In voodoo (or vodoun), a mysterious tradition with African origins, there are thousands of gods. Often in contact with humans, some of these gods are served by millions, some are honored by only one family, and some have been forgotten.[873] Known as *lwa* or *loa,* they have a variety of personalities, from the severe power of Ogou, the god of fire, war, iron, and machinery,[873] to the mischief of Baron Samedi, who can be puckish and obscene.[873, 229]

The lwa are distinguished from men by their power and knowledge, but in most respects they are like humans. They are wily, lascivious, sensitive, jealous, and temperamental.[584]

Voodoo teaches that the lwa are constantly in contact with our world. They mainly communicate through dreams and through possessions that occur during voodoo rituals. People who are possessed during sleep will remember the experience. People who are possessed while awake will not remember.[584]

Human contact with the lwa is so common that Alfred Metraux made this observation: "The ubiquity of the *loa* and their incarnations are the objects of beliefs so profound and so unquestioned that possessions are received with less fuss than the arrival of a friend."[584]

Remarkably, the lwa may even appear physically to humans in broad daylight,[584] with Zaka being the lwa who most often reveals himself in "concrete form." He typically is seen as a peasant in a blue shirt, and he often limps. He may ask you for rum and cassava. Those who are wise will not refuse a god.[584]

No complete list of the lwa is possible because new ones are always being created "in popular faith" and others are "forgotten for want of devotees."[584] Without devotees and sacrifices, the lwa weaken and fade away.[584, 873]

How does one become a voodoo god or goddess?

People famous or infamous in life are automatically elevated to the status of lwa after death. This includes François Duvalier (1907–1971),[584, 873, 217] the fearsome dictator and voodoo sorcerer, John Fitzgerald Kennedy (1917–1963), the American president killed exactly one year after a Duvalier death hex,[948] and Jean-Jacques Dessalines (1758–1806), who went from being a slave to the emperor of Haiti before being killed by his own people.[584, 873, 217]

Voodoo priests and priestesses also become lwa after death, especially the priests and priestesses who have many followers. Marie Laveau (1801–1881) of New Orleans, the celebrated voodoo priestess, is now a goddess.[338, 873]

DIE FOR THE EMPEROR OF JAPAN
AND BECOME A JAPANESE GOD

Motoori Norinaga (1730–1801) famously called Japan the land of eight million gods, but in reality the number is infinite.[616, 651] Called the *kami,* the gods reside not only in paradise, but also everywhere on earth, including mountains, rivers, and private homes.[743]

The Japanese people sometimes encounter these gods. When seen, a kami most commonly appears as a snake or as an old man with a white beard and long white hair who is dressed in white.[86] When one of the kami arrives, a human may hear footsteps.[86]

At the Yasukuni shrine in central Tokyo—a shrine sacred in the Shinto religion—those who have died for Japan in war have their spirits transformed into kami through rituals. The kami made there include the famous kamikaze pilots of World War II, and a number of individuals executed by the victorious allies after the same war.[719, 484, 815, 756, 727, 649]

Seeing its war dead as "shattered jewels" and "god-heroes," the Yasukuni shrine is the only place to which the emperor of Japan bows.

REMAIN PURE AND FIND THE HOLY GRAIL

The Holy Grail is the cup from which Jesus drank at his last meal before his arrest and murder. According to legend, the Holy Grail was also used by Joseph of Arimathea to collect Christ's blood at Golgotha, the "place of the skull."[903]

According to medieval lore, the Holy Grail was brought to England, and it gave immortality and eternal youth to those who saw it. If approached by the impure, however, the Holy Grail disappeared.[656, 53]

In the legends, only three knights of King Arthur succeeded in seeing the Holy Grail.[903, 656, 53]

CHANGE YOURSELF

Peter D. Ouspensky (1878–1947) was an eternalist. In other words, he thought that the passage of time was unreal. All times, he believed, exist simultaneously. There is only the "eternal now," the state in which "everything is everywhere always."[656]

To use Ouspensky's own words: "Time does not exist! There exists no perpetual and eternal appearance and disappearance of phenomena, no ceaselessly flowing fountain of ever appearing and ever vanishing events."[656]

When a person dies, wrote Ouspensky, he is immediately reborn into his own life. A man born in 1877 who died in 1912 would at death find himself in 1877: "The soul sinks into sleep, and then awakes in the same world as before, in the same house, with the same parents."[656]

The ordinary man will repeat his life each time exactly.[657] He will marry the same person, he will choose the same profession, and he will die the same way. He will make the same choices because he is the same person in the same circumstances.

Ouspensky thought, however, that an individual with a *strong* soul—someone who has "attained great consciousness and power"— could break free of this eternal repetition by changing *himself.* "You cannot change anything, and nothing will change by itself. . . . In order to change anything you must first change yourself."[657]

A person who manages to change himself will be reincarnated as someone else. This reincarnation can only occur into the past.[656]

Now, this "reincarnation into the past" is possible only into places that have become free, into "vacancies."[656]

A vacancy can occur in two ways. "The first way is when a soul, after many lives of conscious struggle, obtains freedom, leaves the circle of lives in the *particular place in time,* and goes in the direction of its source, that is, into the past."[656]

The second way, according to Ouspensky, is when a soul dies. That is, when "after many lives spent in sliding down an incline, in moving along a diminishing spiral with a quicker and quicker end, a soul ceases to be born." Such degenerate souls disappear. "This is real death," wrote Ouspensky, "for death exists just as life exists."[656]

According to Ouspensky, when a soul reincarnates as someone else, or, when a soul dies, a vacancy occurs. The person in history still exists, however, and another soul takes that person over.[656]

In other words, there will always be a Jefferson Davis, the president of the Confederate States of America. But, in the endless time, different souls may be Jefferson Davis.

Having read this, however, be warned! These are Ouspensky's words:

> But a man who has begun to guess the great secret must make use of it, otherwise it will turn against him. It is not a safe secret. . . . When one finds the secret or hears about it, one has only two or three, or in any case only a few more lives.[657]

COMMIT EVERY POSSIBLE SIN AND INDULGE IN EVERY POSSIBLE EXPERIENCE

Carpocrates of Alexandria founded the Carpocratians, a radical Christian sect, in the first half of the second century. Members, as an identifying mark, are branded in the back parts of the lobe of the right ear.[394, 276]

The Carpocratians claimed that their unusual teachings came from Jesus himself. Jesus, they claim, privately revealed mysteries to his disciples, and these disciples "requested and obtained permission to hand down the things thus taught them, to others who should be worthy."[425]

The Carpocratians believe that the material universe is evil, while the non-material world is good. Accordingly, the ruler of this world, a jealous tyrant, is malevolent, and he is linked to this material world. He thinks he is god, but he is not. The true god is the ineffable one, a being of light.[406]

The soul, according to the Carpocratians, is trapped in a physical body, like a pearl embedded in filth. Moral laws keep the soul captive, and the only way to achieve liberation from the misery of rebirth is to defy these laws by experiencing everything the body can experience.[569]

True to their teachings, the Carpocratians scorn moral laws and indulge in every possible activity, including vice. They experience orgies and sexual perversions because, in their opinion, "the various things that men consider evil are not evil."[276, 412]

Ultimately, after everything has been experienced, the soul is released from its bodily prison and ascended to the ineffable god of light.[394]

This release could be attained during one lifetime or over several lifetimes.[394, 406]

SALVATION THROUGH SCIENCE

Reconstruct and Repair the Corpse

Nikolai Fyodorovich Fyodorov (sometimes Anglicized as "Fedorov"), lived from 1827 to 1903. A thoroughgoing materialist, he believed that we could scientifically resurrect the dead.[711]

Just as a broken clock will function when the parts are reassembled correctly, Fyodorov believed that if we reconstituted a dead body's material components in the *correct* way, it would become animate. Put together the engine, he said, and the consciousness would return.[711]

Very literally, Fyodorov wanted to develop technology to resurrect dead ancestors.[711]

Salvation by Ice

In the eighteenth century, John Hunter (1728–1793) hoped to prolong the life of man indefinitely through freezing and thawing. His own research involved the freezing and thawing of animals.[312]

Since water-bears and wood frogs can be frozen and revived, and so can human embryos and sperm, the idea is not outlandish.[103]

In the modern era, the idea was popularized by Robert C. W. Ettinger (1918–2011), a professor at Wayne State University, who published *The Prospect of Immortality* in 1962. The book fostered what became known as the Immortalist movement.[283]

According to Robert Ettinger, "Being born is not a crime, so why must it carry a sentence of death?"[424]

The first freezing of a human under controlled conditions was performed on Dr. James H. Bedford, a retired psychologist, in January 1967.[463]

At the time of writing, 1,000 people have signed contracts to be frozen. Sometimes the entire body is treated, but some choose to have only their heads frozen.[424]

Be Cloned by Extraterrestrials

The Raelian movement was founded in 1974 after Claude Vorilhon, later known as Rael, encountered a bus-sized spacecraft and a 25,000-year-old alien named Yahweh. Rael, who claims he is the son of Yahweh (through artificial insemination), also claims he is the half-brother of Jesus, Mohammad, the Buddha, and thirty-six other messengers.[709, 667]

Rael claims he has visited the home planet of the aliens, whom he refers to as the Elohim. Elohim, Rael notes, means "those who came from the sky."[709, 667]

Rael denies the existence of god or a soul, and he insists that the only possible immortality is regeneration through the science of cloning.

(Yahweh himself, claims Rael, has been cloned twenty-five times.)[709, 667] Clones are not uncommon—all identical twins are clones—but Rael claims that the Elohim can preserve an individual's memory and personality and can deposit them in his new body. Through this technology, death can be mastered.[709, 667, 526]

Presently, the Elohim have plans to clone earthlings. According to Rael, the aliens will clone only the most worthy humans, and they bestow this boon on the basis of service.[709, 667, 526]

The followers of Rael arrange to have a piece of bone (one square centimeter in size) cut from their foreheads after death. This bone, which Rael calls the "third eye," is preserved in a secure vault.[709, 667, 526] The Elohim, the Raelians believe, can reconstitute the complete individual from that bone.[709, 667, 526]

HAUNT UNTIL YOU BECOME A GOD

Sagawara Michizane, who lived CE 845–903 in Japan, was a scholar, poet, and politician. A victim of injustice, he was sent into exile, and he died in disgrace.[86, 599]

After death, Sagawara Michizane avenged himself. Japan experienced a number of calamities, including flood, drought, lightning, and plague; these disasters were attributed to his angry ghost.[86]

To placate his specter, the Japanese honored Sagawara Michizane as a Tenjin or "heavenly deity."

Now venerated as the Shinto god of scholarship, many shrines in Japan are dedicated to him, including a great one in Kyoto.[599, 86, 719]

CALL UPON AMIDA BUDDHA AND
SPEAK THESE WORDS: *NAMU AMIDA BUTSU*

Religions are often founded by gods. For example, the ancient Etruscans of Italy received their religion from a mysterious child-sized being who emerged from a freshly ploughed field, dictated the sacred books to the people, and then died.[166, 658, 220, 437] Buddhism, however, is a religion without priests, and it is not based on revelation. The Buddha

(563–483 BCE) was not the prophet or emissary of a god, and he rejected the idea of a "God-Supreme being."[261]

Acting alone, the Buddha achieved enlightenment at the age of thirty-five, after six years of concentrated study, yogic discipline, and meditative contemplation. Writing on this awakening, Professor W. Scott Morton observed:

> It is to be noted that no dependence on a personal god was involved and that his experience seems to have been in the nature of a psychological breakthrough, in which he arrived at an intuitive understanding of suffering and life as a whole.[601]

From the warrior caste in India, the Buddha, who was born Siddhartha Gautama, could walk and talk from birth.[535] Raised as a "cloistered prince"—his father shielded him from the sight of all suffering—he secretly left the palace and was shocked when he encountered the old, the sick, and the dying. Horrified, he renounced his parents, his wife, his child, and all possessions to seek the solution to the problem of human misery.[70, 535]

He practiced austerities and meditated with sages, but failed to find the answer. At last, on the verge of starvation, he resolved not to move until he found the knowledge he sought. This led to enlightenment. He became the Buddha, the "awakened one."[535]

Buddhism teaches that rebirth is caused by three poisons: love, hatred, and delusion.[208, 533, 662, 535] Until we are free from love (clinging to material things), hatred (the desire to avoid or destroy things that interfere with happiness), and delusion (the mistaken view that the material world represents ultimate reality), we will continue to be reborn and we will continue to suffer for millions and millions of lives.[662, 305, 70, 665]

After the Buddha's death, Buddhism spread and was modified by each country that it entered. Western scholars are often critical of these changes—Marco Pallis (1895–1989) noted that a "Protestant" influence leads us to study other religions with a prejudice favoring "unalterable adherence to an earlier practice"[665]—but the fact is that living religions do indeed change.

Some important types of Buddhism are Theravada (Hinayana tradition), the Tibetan Right-Handed Tantric Vajrayana (Diamond Vehicle tradition), and Sino-Japanese Mahayana (including Pure Land Buddhism).[70]

In Theravada Buddhism, nirvana, or escape from the cycle of rebirth and redeath, is reached through meditation, discipline, and moral living. To be moral, one should be a "blessing to the world."[281, 70]

Another form of Buddhism, Diamond Vehicle Buddhism, uses esoteric methods and rituals to evade the effects of karma and achieve liberation in one lifetime. As previously noted, the *Bardo Thodal,* the *Tibetan Book of the Dead,* is a product of this type of Buddhism.[70]

Mahayana Buddhism, a third school, offers salvation through a kind of Buddha savior entity.[70, 139] Pure Land Buddhism belongs to Mahayana Buddhism, and the savior entity is the Amida Buddha.

Who Is Amida Buddha?

Amitabha, who is called Amida Buddha in Japan, is *not* an incarnation of Siddhartha Gautama (the best-known Buddha), but was a monk named Dharmakara.[535]

This monk, who lived "long ago" in "a universe far away," is responsible for a Pure Land that exists here and now and is open to all who would seek it.[535, 834]

In the Mahayana tradition, there are many Buddhas, and each has a Pure Land. Indeed, there are an infinite number of Buddhas, and an infinite number of Buddha lands (called "Buddha fields"). The Buddha lands are "created by the merits or thoughts of the saviors."[261]

(Interestingly, from the Mahayana perspective, even the paradise of Christ can be perceived as a Buddha realm.)[139]

When the Amida Buddha achieved enlightenment, he became a bodhisattva, or one who refuses to enter nirvana until all sentient beings also enter nirvana.[261, 665] This pure act of compassion by the

Amida Buddha brought a paradise, a "Pure Land," into existence.[637]

How is that possible? It is an Indian idea that when one attains spiritual perfection, the place where one is situated also changes. This is because the universe is a mental construction, like a dream.[535] In the words of the *Dhammapada,* an early Buddhist text, "All things are led by thought, are controlled by thought, are made up by thought."[120, 834, 233]

And, since "mind-only" Buddhism teaches that only thought exists, this Pure Land thought place of the Amida Buddha is as real as this world and we may go there.[535, 637]

Entering Paradise

In Pure Land Buddhism, all are welcome in Amida's paradise. No one is excluded because of weakness, misconduct, or deficiency.[792] All that is needed is absolute trust in the Buddha. To gain entry, one needs to call on the Amida Buddha only once.[792, 535]

As expressed by one modern Shin Buddhist (Shin Buddhism is a Pure Land Sect in Japan), "Amida is willing to save us as we are, ignorant and sinful." Very literally, "all who believe in Amida and his will to save will surely be born in the Land of Happiness."[9]

A land of bliss, the Pure Land of Amida Buddha is forever enduring and radiant.[139] It is a place of enchanting colors, jeweled mountains, harmonious sounds, and fragrance. Everyone in the Pure Land experiences peaceful calm. No evil can exist there. There is no sickness or death. There are no rules or conflicts. Food is abundant but unnecessary.[70, 792, 342, 176]

The Pure Land is outside the wheel of rebirth, but it is not nirvana, the ultimate goal. Technically, the Pure Land is NOT a permanent paradise, but an ideal environment for meditation and practice where one can achieve enlightenment and (eventually) nirvana.[70, 637, 139]

Indeed, in the Pure Land, attaining nirvana is assured.[70] People in the Pure Land will attain enlightenment without struggle against great obstacles.[834]

So how may one enter this Pure Land? Remarkably, it can be attained with a single thought or a few words.[261, 834]

As promised in the *Larger Sutra,* a sacred text of Pure Land Buddhism, anyone who calls the name of Amida Buddha—anyone who has "meditated on me with serene thoughts at the moment of death"—will be granted happiness in this Pure Land.[70, 9, 535, 834, 342, 603]

To call on the Amida Buddha in Japanese, say *Namu Amida Butsu.* In Chinese, say the phrase *A-mi-t'o-fo.* In English, say *I take refuge in the Buddha of Immeasurable Life and Light.*[792]

Since you do not know when you will die, you should repeat the name of Amida Buddha often. While chanting *Namu Amida Butsu,* think of nothing else.[792]

DIE WITH NOBLE THOUGHTS

The Buddha in the *Mahakamma-Vibhanga Sutra* states that both previous deeds and final thoughts influence rebirth. Since bad men sometimes have noble thoughts as they die, and good men sometimes have wicked thoughts, that would explain why bad men are sometimes born into good situations and vice versa.[70]

So a god in our time could have been a felon in his last life?

Yes, and the reasons follow . . .

In Buddhism, every intentional act, whether in thought, word, or deed, leaves a "residue" in the doer. This residue will eventually produce an effect. This is called karma.[536]

In the words of Marco Pallis, "every activity, be it the most trivial or apparently purposeless; sets in motion, as cause, a new series of effects."[665]

Thus, no right action, no matter how "quixotic," is useless and no foolish action, no matter how insignificant, is harmless.[665]

In effect, even a thought can change the world.[665]

DIE WITH A GOOD STATE OF MIND

As Professor Donald S. Lopez explains, in Buddhism, your next rebirth is NOT determined by the cumulative effect of good and evil deeds committed in this life. Instead, *one* deed, completed in *one* of your countless former lives, can serve as a cause for an *entire* lifetime.[536]

Since each individual has many karmic seeds, which one will determine the next life? Buddhism teaches that the state of mind at death will determine the next life.[536]

If one dies with a positive state of mind (such as devotion to the Buddha), a virtuous deed done in the past will serve as the cause of the next life. As a result, the individual will be reborn as a human or a god.[536] (A previous act of generosity results in rebirth as a god.)[536]

On the other hand, if there is a negative state of mind at death (such as attachment to possessions, friends, or loved ones), a "non-virtuous" deed from the past will serve as the cause of the next lifetime, and the individual will be reborn as an animal, a hungry ghost, or hellish being.[536]

BECOME A GREAT SAGE
AND ACQUIRE A RAINBOW BODY

The Diamond Vehicle (or Thunderbolt Vehicle)[535] Buddhists of Tibet say that when exceptionally great sages die, they do not leave behind a corpse.[820, 340]

Instead, accomplished sages, at the time of death, will dissolve their bodies into rainbow bodies and leave nothing behind except their hair and nails. This is a sign of enlightenment.[533, 87, 340]

According to Lama A-Chos, a renowned Buddhist, it requires approximately sixty years of intensive practice to achieve the rainbow body.[928]

In the twentieth century, several individuals reputedly attained a rainbow body, including Khenpo A-Chos (in 1998)[928] and Sonam Namgyal (in 1952). Sonam Namgyal reportedly attained the rainbow body in front of thousands of people.[546]

David Steindl-Rast, a German scholar, and Father Francis Tiso, an ordained Roman Catholic priest, have both studied the rainbow body.

Since Jesus's tomb was empty on Easter morning, Father Tiso has suggested that Jesus may have left the earth in a "rainbow body."[928]

TAKE OVER ANOTHER HUMAN BODY
(A FRESH CORPSE)

Helena Blavatsky (1831–1891), a Russian occultist and a scholar of eso-terica, referred to a "last and dreaded rite" of the voluntary transfer of life from one man to another. In effect, a master adept, whose body has been worn out by age, transfers his consciousness to a young body.[90]

The process was used in "Thing on the Doorstep," a horror story by H. P. Lovecraft (1890–1937). In that tale a wizard transposes his mind with the mind of his daughter. While inhabiting the body of his daughter, the wizard marries a weak-willed young man to take that man's body.[879]

Although Lovecraft was writing fiction, in the East the technique is viewed as real. It is found in both Hinduism and Tibetan Buddhism.

Hindus call it Parakaya Pravesha. A yogic practice, it is the tech-nique of leaving a body without dying and entering another body with-out being reborn. This usually refers to entering a fresh corpse to bring it back to life.[266, 442]

Sir John George Woodroffe (1865–1936), an Oxford-educated Englishman and the chief justice of the Calcutta Supreme Court in British-ruled India, saw an old man—an adept—perform the ritual. The apparent result: the adept dropped his own elderly body and took possession of the body of young man whose corpse was being prepared for cremation.[442]

Shocked by what he had seen, Woodroffe devoted the rest of his life to the study of the arcane lore of the Tantra. Publishing under the pseudonym of Arthur Avalon, his books are the best available (in English) in Tantric studies.[442]

Of course, if taking over the body of a young person is possible, why do we not see the process more often? Because, say the Hindus, when a yogi takes over another body, it still has its ex-owner's habits and desires. Besides, why take a used body, when one can be reborn fresh and new as a baby?[442]

In Tibet, mind-transference is called *powa* or *pho-wa*. The art of taking over someone else's new dead body is called *grong-jug*.[820, 363]

As in India, the consciousness is emptied from one individual and introduced into a second body that has been previously emptied of consciousness. When performed, there is no death, no time in the bardo state, and no rebirth.[207]

There are many different powa practices,[363] but one interesting technique is described by Alexandra David-Neel (1868–1969). According to David-Neel, when an *adept* shouts the syllable *hick* three times in the *correct* tone, followed by the syllable *phat* (pronounced like "peth"), also in the *correct* tone, it causes the consciousness to gush from the crown of the head. The consciousness can then enter a destination of its choice. This could be another body or a Pure Land.[207]

The syllables must be pronounced precisely, and the pronunciation must be learned from a master. A long apprenticeship is required.[207]

The student must never pronounce the hick with the phat until he is ready to use them. Speaking the syllables around a dying person will cause that individual to die. If the student speaks the syllables together when he is alone, he will die.[207, 533]

AS YOU DIE,
THINK OF A HINDU GOD OR HIS AVATAR

As Professor Klaus K. Klostermaier notes in his splendid books, Hinduism has three *main* paths. All paths agree that we are not born free, but we must liberate ourselves through discipline.[487]

The first path, called *karmamarga,* is the path of works. It presupposes a high-caste standing.[487]

The second path, called *jnanamarga,* is the path of knowledge. It is for scholars.[487]

The third path, called *bhaktimarga,* is the path of loving devotion. It promises salvation to anyone, including low-caste people, women and children, and brute animals.[487]

The third path, a kind of devotional theism, was expounded for the first time in the Bhagavad Gita, a Hindu classic. Here, release from rebirth was a divine gift to the faithful. Other methods require striving, penance, and pain, but bhaktimarga is an easy shortcut.[487, 637]

How does this work?

Hinduism, like all Indian religions, teaches that a dying man's thoughts determine his future status.[63, 120] The Bhagavad Gita, makes this idea clear: "For on whomsoever one thinks at the last moment of life, unto him in truth he goes, through sympathy with his nature."[80]

Thus, the *Padma Purana* tells of a man frightened by demons at the moment of death, and because he thought of demons he was reborn as one.[120]

In the Bhagavad Gita, Krishna, who is an avatar of the god Vishnu (an avatar is a manifestation of a god on earth), promises that whoever thinks of him at death will find him. These are the words: "And he who at the end of his time leaves his body thinking of me, he in truth comes to my being: he in truth comes to me."[80]

Interestingly, the soul released through *bhaktimarga* does not merge with an impersonal Brahman, but could individually enjoy an *afterlife* of devotion to a god such as Vishnu or Shiva, in a paradise.[637]

As the sage Ramakrishna (1836–1886) said, "I want to taste sugar, not become sugar."[637]

THROUGHOUT LIFE, CHANT HOLY MANTRAS

A mantra, which may consist of words or sounds alone,[481] can be recited silently or uttered aloud.[481] A mantra has power over gods. A mantra also has power over karma, something that is more powerful than gods.[535, 487]

In India, one famous mantra is the Maha Mrityunjaya, the "Great Death-Conquering Mantra."[442] It is addressed to "the three-eyed one," an epithet of the god named Rudra, who is also called Shiva.[487] It is said to prolong life and to take the person to Shiva at death.[442]

The Great Death-Conquering Mantra is a verse from the *Rig Veda*

(7.59.12). (According to the Hindus, all the hymns in the Vedas are mantric in nature.)[295, 481] In English, this is the mantra: "I honor the All-Seeing One, whose grace is all-pervading like the fragrance of a flower. May he release me from the grip of death as easily as ripe fruit is released from the vine."[728]

FOLLOW THE PATH OF SMOKE
OR THE PATH OF FIRE

Hinduism has the doctrine of the path of smoke (rebirth) and the path of fire (release from rebirth and redeath). Both paths are legitimate, but the path of fire is superior. The paths are discussed in the *Brihadaranyaka Upanishad*.[117, 139, 238, 487, 202]

The path of smoke leads to the moon, the "fathers" (ancestors), and rebirth. To follow this path, live among people and practice faith, almsgiving, and austerities (such as fasting and celibacy). (In Hinduism, asceticism probably began as shamanistic ordeals performed to achieve magical powers.)[63] The goal of the path of smoke is rebirth at a higher level.[139, 238, 117, 487]

The path of fire leads to the sun and the gods and release from rebirth and redeath. To follow the path of fire, go to the "forest" (wilderness) and meditate.[139, 238]

There are three types of meditation:[826]

1. "Concentration on One Point." With this technique, focus the mind on a chosen object, such as a bowl of water. Fix it in your mind, so you can see it, even when your eyes are closed.[208]
2. "Bring thinking to a standstill."[826]
3. "Raja Yoga." With this technique, witness the free flow of mind without interference, and without censuring guidance.[826]

COPY THE *LOTUS SUTRA*

The *Lotus Sutra* is an important religious text in Mahayana Buddhism. The *Lotus Sutra* states that anyone who copies it—even without reading or reciting it—will be reborn in their next life as a god in the "Heaven of the Thirty-Three."[535]

It is interesting that some pious Buddhists will copy the "Guanyin" (chapter 25 of the *Lotus Sutra*) in their own blood.[535]

SAVE AN ANIMAL FROM THE BUTCHER

Considered a meritorious Buddhist practice, purchasing live animals destined for the dinner table and releasing them gives a person longevity, prosperity, progeny, freedom from mental illness, and rebirth in a heavenly realm.[535]

DIE FROM WATER

To the Aztecs of central Mexico, Tlaloc was a god of rain, lightning, thunder, and vegetation. In the city of Tenochtitlan, Tlaloc shared the main temple with the gods Quetzalcoatl and Huitzilopochtli.[808, 150]

Like other Aztec deities, Tlaloc required human sacrifice, and priests sacrificed children to him during the dry season. According to tradition, if the victims cried during the proceedings, their tears were a sign of the plentiful rain to come.[226, 176, 718]

One level of the Aztec afterlife was named Tlalocan after the god. Located above the moon,[726, 171, 381] it was a green place of flowers and warm rain. The souls of the dead who were sacred to Tlaloc—victims of drowning, lightning, and certain "water" diseases such as dropsy or pustules—went to this lush garden paradise. Their bodies, which were never cremated, were painted blue and buried with dried wood.[523, 226, 176, 312]

All the dead who went to Tlaloc remained with him for four years only. After four years, they were reborn on earth.[523, 226]

DRINK WATER FROM THE RIVER STYX

According to the historian Herodotus, the river named Styx (meaning "hated")[354] came to the surface of the earth in the town of Nonacris, which is in Arcadia, near the town of Pheneus. At that location, one could see a small stream trickling from a rock.[354, 389]

According to the ancient Greeks, the water of the river ruins all matter: it is inimical to glass, metal, stone, and any container. Only the hoof of a horse or a mule resists it.[227, 678]

The water is lethal to men except one day each year, when it becomes the water of immortality. Unfortunately, no one knows which day the water of death becomes the water of immortality.[227]

Pausanias (110–180 CE), the Greek writer, said he heard a story that Alexander the Great (the Zoroastrians call him Alexander the "Damned")[826, 630] was poisoned with Styx water. Alexander died—just before his thirty-third birthday—on June 11, 323 BCE.[678]

UNDERGO THE ORDEAL OF FIRE

Marie Vietroff, a student in tsarist Russia, was arrested in 1896 because of a forbidden book in her room. After a month of ghastly abuse and ill-treatment in "Peter and Paul Fortress," including rape, she committed suicide by burning herself to death.[937]

Her fiery death was a pointless end to a tragic life.

Or was it?

In India, the Hindus say that burying oneself in cakes of dried cow dung and setting fire to oneself will lead to liberation. This method, which is considered very meritorious, is called Karjhagni.[487] (Since cow dung enriches the soil and provides fuel for fire, it is considered sacred in India. On some occasions the goddess Sri is worshipped in the form of cow dung. This is enjoined in *Nilalata Purana*.)[481, 631]

The Puranas state that whoever dies in the city of Prayaga (Allahabad), naturally or through suicide, is sure to obtain liberation, so the burning should take place there.[487]

In the Western world, meanwhile, members of the Order of the Solar Temple believe that suicide and fire will allow them to "transit" in glorious "solar bodies" with "all lucidity and in full consciousness" to a place called Proxima, a planet that orbits Sirius, the "Blue Star."[527]

To take on a solar body, the Solar Temple teaches that we must first "depose" the mortal body. The transit must be done in the least violent way possible. To keep the deceased from losing his way in transit and returning to the physical body, the body must be burned.[527]

Dressed in occult robes, many members of the Solar Temple died in groups in 1994, 1995, and 1997. The group suicides occurred at the time of the equinoxes or the solstices.[527]

Before leaving the earth, members of the Solar Temple decided to drive a stake through the heart of a three-month-old baby named Emanuelle Dutoit. The child, they believed, was the Anti-Christ.[527] Gerry Genoud, who performed the actual murder, believed that he was a reincarnation of the Roman soldier who had lanced Jesus on the cross. Genoud believed that to expiate his crime against the Christ, he must kill the Anti-Christ.[527]

In documents left behind in 1994, members declared that "we will continue to work in other places, in other times." Having left earth, members said they would wait for "circumstances favorable to a possible return."[527]

Members believe that they have returned repeatedly throughout history to contribute to the evolution of mankind.[527]

The Solar Temple draws inspiration from the medieval Templars, dozens of whom were tortured and burned alive at the stake in the fourteenth century.[527]

LEAP INTO AN ACTIVE VOLCANO

In Japan, Mount Mihara is an active volcano on the remote island of Izu Oshima. According to legend, a person who leaps into the volcano is instantly cremated and his soul goes to a heaven in a plume of smoke. In 1933, at least 133 suicides occurred there. In 1936, 619 suicides occurred there.[824]

DO NOT BE CREMATED OR EMBALMED

According to Robert Crookall (1890–1981), a botanist and geologist who was interested in afterlife research, "death is essentially a birth,"[188] and the nature of the death determines the experience. Crookall claimed that a violent death in battle is like a Caesarian section, and death from old age is like a natural birth.[188]

Crookall claimed that in life a silver cord—a kind of umbilical cord—connects the soul to the body. When the cord breaks, death occurs.[188] This silver cord is mentioned in the Bible, in the twelfth chapter of Ecclesiastes.[188]

According to Crookall, the person who is conscious during death will feel no pain. He will feel that he is rising above the body or falling below it.[188]

Some, however, will black out as the soul disengages, and this will feel like falling asleep or being given an anesthetic.[188]

Crookall claimed that a "second death" will occur three to four days after the first death. During this second death, the soul will shed something that he called the "vehicle of vitality." Crookall said this vehicle of vitality corresponds to the afterbirth in childbirth. Once shed, it remains behind, like a kind of astral shell or astral corpse.[188]

Crookall warned people not to cremate. Cremation, he claimed, caused a violent and possibly premature separation of the "vehicle of vitality" and the soul.[188]

He also warned people not to embalm the dead or to place them in metal coffins. These actions, he wrote, would retard the separation of the vehicle of vitality from soul body.[188]

He recommended burial in an ordinary wooden coffin that permits natural decomposition.[188]

UNDERGO THE ORDEAL OF CASTRATION

When Jesus was tempted in the desert, the devil did not tempt him with a woman.[656] The Christ, the Bible seems to say, was beyond carnal lust.

Jesus taught his followers the value of castration, and he recommends the practice in the Gospel of Matthew (19:12):

For there are some eunuchs, which were so born from their mother's womb: and there are some eunuchs, which were made eunuchs of men: and there be eunuchs, which have made themselves eunuchs for the kingdom of heaven's sake. He that is able to receive it, let him receive it.

Tertullian of Carthage (circa 160–220 CE), an early church father, described Jesus himself and Paul of Tarsus as eunuchs,[855] and Origen (184/185–253/254 CE), another church father, castrated himself in the interest of piety.[284] An early Christian sect, the Valerians, also embraced the practice.[556, 495]

In the eighteenth century, a mysterious man that history knows as Konratti Selivanov (died, officially at least, in 1832), appeared to spread the "good news of castration." Selivanov claimed that he was Christ returned.[385]

The followers of Selivanov call themselves the Purists or the White Doves. Outsiders call them the Skoptsy (or Skoptzy).[556]

The Skoptsy do not recognize the Bible (they call it the "Dead Bible"), and they believe that the real Bible is their holy book, the "Book of the Dove."[556]

Members swear strict oaths of secrecy,[870, 275] and they claim they are the only true Christians. Their conventicles for worship include frenzied dancing.[870, 556]

They do not smoke tobacco, drink alcohol, or eat meat. They survive on vegetables, milk, and fish.[556]

According to the Skoptsy, the first sin was the sexual intercourse of Adam and Eve. They believe that the vagina is the abyss and the penis is the key to the abyss.[275, 318]

Jesus, they say, preached castration, castrated himself, and all of his disciples did the same. With time, however, decadence in the church—especially under the emperor named Constantine (circa 272–337 CE)—perverted the true faith, and the practice disappeared.[556]

The Skoptsy teach that castration, which "whitens" the body and the soul, is the way of salvation.[870] Those who are "sealed," as they call it, upon death go to the "House of God."[556]

Referred to as "baptism by fire" (John the Baptist promised that the Messiah would "baptize with fire"), their sacrament of castration was originally performed with a red-hot iron. Later, a knife was used, and fire was used to cauterize the wound.[556, 275, 870] In some cases, the person is tied to a rough frame in the form of a cross.[556]

Men in the sect subject themselves to the "Minor Seal" (removing the testes) and the "Major Seal" (removing the penis). For women, in the Minor Seal the nipples are removed, and in the Major Seal the breasts, clitoris, and labia are removed.[318, 556, 275]

Although the sect is small, members look forward to the establishment of an "empire of the pure." They believe that this will occur when the Skoptsy—the people who are sealed—number 144,000, the special number mentioned in the Book of Revelation.[556, 275]

ABSTAIN FROM ALL SEX

Mother Ann Lee (1736–1784) was the leader of the United Society of Believers in Christ's Second Appearing, the people popularly known as Shakers. During her brief life, she was incarcerated and brutalized.[142]

Shakers believe that the second coming of Christ occurred in the eighteenth century. With the first manifestation, during Roman times, the Christ filled the man Jesus. With the second manifestation, during the Age of Enlightenment, the Christ filled the woman named Ann Lee.[142, 921]

Shakers do not worship Jesus or Mother Ann Lee, but emulate them.[142] Both Jesus the Nazarene and Mother Ann Lee possess the Christ spirit, but neither is a god.[142]

At the age of thirty-four years, while in prison, Mother Ann Lee had a powerful vision. It was revealed to her that sex causes our separation from god. Sex is the source of all human ills, and sex was the sin that caused Adam and Eve to lose paradise.[142]

According to Mother Ann Lee, "only through celibacy can true Godliness be achieved."[21, 142]

Shakers follow a pure Christian life. They take literally the words of Jesus in Matthew V:18: "Be ye perfect even as your Father in heaven is perfect."

Shakers live simply in egalitarian communities where all men and women are equal and where all work and wealth are shared. Shakers work from dawn to dusk, pausing at regular intervals for worship.[142, 21]

In their communities, the genders are strictly separated. Men and women are never allowed to be alone. Touching is never allowed, and even shaking hands is forbidden.[142]

New members are gained through conversions and the adoption of orphans. When orphans are adopted, they are free to leave the commune—and the Shaker faith—when they reach adulthood.[142]

Refusing to swear oaths or bear arms, they reject clergy, creeds, liturgies, and sacraments.[21, 142] Their worship services are joyous occasions featuring rhythmic singing and festive dancing.[142]

Famous for their hard work and frugality, there were 6,000 Shakers holding 100,000 acres of farmland in common in 1845, but now only a few members remain.

This was predicted by Mother Ann Lee: "There will come a time when there won't be enough Believers to bury their own dead. When only five are left, then there will be a revival."[142]

SURVIVE THE ORDEAL OF THE WILD FRUIT

In many traditions, we are told that as souls journey to the next world, they are tormented by hunger or thirst. Thirst features in the Orphic Mysteries. Hunger as an ordeal is found among the Ojibway nation, an Indian people located near Lake Superior.

According to the Ojibway, on the path that souls must follow, wild strawberries grow.[9] The souls will feel great hunger, but they must master their craving. For whoever eats the strawberries will die a second death.[9]

JOIN A SECRET SOCIETY

The Winnebago, a Native American nation in North America, believe that a whole series of reincarnations on earth are secured by participating in the medicine society, a kind of secret society.[708, 414]

As Professor Joscelyn Godwin notes, "Secrecy is out of favor in our times, because of the official fiction that everyone is equal, hence entitled to the same information," but that was not always the case.[340]

BE KILLED BY LIGHTNING

Summer is the season of lightning,[809] but lightning strikes the earth *somewhere* 100 times each second.[824, 880]

When lightning targets a human, the result can be spectacular in a terrifying way. In 114 BCE, lightning struck a young girl on horseback, and it stripped her naked and obliterated her tongue.[872]

Seeing such power, the ancient Greeks treated anything struck by lightning with reverence, and people killed by lightning were honored. Their bodies were not buried or cremated, but were left where they were. Those killed by lightning included Semele and Capaneus.[111, 695, 314]

Likewise, the Zulu of South Africa say that people killed by lightning are with the god of the sky. (People who die of other causes reside under the dark earth.) The lightning-killed people are buried where they lie. No mourning for them is permitted and they are never discussed.[514]

In the modern Western world, one noted lightning strike occurred in 1975, when Dannion Brinkley was struck while speaking on the telephone. Although Brinkley survived, he called the experience a "phone call from god."[119]

The lightning struck him behind the ear and traveled through his body. Incredibly, so much power was unleashed that the nails in his shoes were welded to the floor.[119]

Declared dead, Brinkley had a life review. Then he saw crystal buildings and beings of light.[119]

"Is this heaven?" he asked, but the beings of light did not reply.[119]

HIRE A SIN-EATER

Bertram S. Puckle, writing in his *Funeral Customs,* describes the sin-eater as a "human scapegoat" who was paid money to "take upon himself the moral trespasses of his client—and whatever the consequences might be in the afterlife—in return for a miserable fee and a scanty meal."[702]

According to Professor Howlett Evans, who saw a sin-eater ritual in a remote part of Britain in 1825, the people treated the sin-eater as a pariah, but when a death occurred, they sought him out.[702]

A simple ritual was performed over the corpse by the sin-eater. By eating some bread, drinking some ale, and uttering a simple prayer, the sin-eater took on the sins of the deceased.[702]

Of course, when the sin-eater himself died, his soul, blackened by sin, was in peril of damnation, but his family could cleanse such sins by hiring another sin-eater.

BECOME A ROMAN CATHOLIC

Traditionally, the Roman Catholic Church taught that *only* Catholics attained salvation. In 1215, the Fourth Lateran Council proclaimed the doctrine of *extra ecclesium nulla salus* ("no salvation outside the church").[865]

Also, in 1302, Pope Boniface VIII issued the papal bull *Unam Sanctum:* "Therefore we declare, state, define and pronounce that it is altogether necessary to salvation for every human creature to be subject to the Roman pontiff."[246]

In the twentieth century, these doctrines were modified by Vatican II, which met from 1962 to 1965. Now the papacy teaches that good people can achieve salvation if they did not have the opportunity to hear the gospel.[865]

These are the words of the modified teaching:

> Those individuals who for no fault of their own do not know the Gospel of Christ and his Church, yet still search for God with an upright heart and try to fulfill his will as recognized in the commands of conscience, in deeds prompted by the working of his grace, can attain eternal salvation.[86, 54]

BURY YOUR DEAD BABY
UNDER THE FLOOR

The Andaman Islanders, who live on islands in the Bay of Bengal, between India and Burma, are an archaic people. Following a way of life that reaches back to the dawn of humanity, they have endured so many eons that—long ago—they forgot how to create fire. They could protect it, but they could not create it.[179] Interestingly, suicide is unknown among them.[526]

When young children die, the Andaman Islanders bury their bodies under the floor, so that their souls can reenter their mothers' wombs and be reborn.[313]

BECOME A GOD, AND WITH
YOUR GODDESS, REIGN OVER YOUR CHILDREN

In the Gospel of John (10:34), Jesus makes this declaration: "Is it not written in your Law, 'I said, you are gods'?"

Jesus was quoting Psalm 82:6: "I said, 'You are gods; you are all sons of the Most High.'"

According to the Church of Jesus Christ of Latter-Day Saints (Mormons), founded by a modern prophet named Joseph Smith, Jr. (1805–1844), there are a vast number of gods and a vast number of inhabited worlds.[570, 146] All of these gods were humans who went through a process called "exaltation" to become gods.[74, 570, 726]

The god of *this* world—the one the Mormons call God the Father and the only God whom they worship[570]—is from a world called Kolob.[74, 801, 301] For the Christian God to be from somewhere is not unusual. According to the Bible, specifically Habakkuk 3:3, "God came from Teman."

Bruce R. McConkie, a Mormon scholar, noted that just as "God used to be a man on another planet,"[570, 74] and became a god, so may we. As Lorenzo Snow, the fifth president of the Latter-Day Saints, famously said: "As man now is, God once was; as God now is, man may be."[74]

According to the Mormons, exaltation is possible only through the

Mormon faith.[726] One must be initiated by baptism, properly performed; one must receive the Holy Ghost by the laying on of "authoritative hands," one must undergo certain secret rituals and swear solemn oaths in a Mormon Temple;[947] one must observe all moral commandments; and one must live a life of cleanliness, purity, and service.[570, 74, 726]

In particular, one must undergo a temple marriage ceremony wherein one marries someone of the opposite gender for *eternity*. Together, the husband and wife will produce spirit children forever in a world where they will reign as a god and a goddess.[570, 74, 726, 301]

Although one must be a Mormon to be exalted, anyone can become a Mormon. Thus, the late Spencer W. Kimball (1895–1985), a Mormon president, could honestly declare: "Each one of you has it within the realm of his possibility to develop a kingship over which you will reside as its king and god."[133]

And, according to the Mormon leader Brigham Young (1801–1877), "The Lord created you and me for the purpose of becoming Gods like Himself."[74, 146]

CONVERT *AFTER* YOU DIE

According to the Church of Jesus Christ of Latter-Day Saints, those who do not accept the gospel in this life will have the opportunity to do so after death. They can receive baptism by proxy. (A living Mormon will be baptized on their behalf.)[800]

According to the Mormons, repentance—even in hell—opens the prison doors to the spirits in hell.[570]

DIE BEFORE
THE AGE OF EIGHT YEARS

According to the *Doctrine and Covenants* of the Mormons, all children who die before the age of eight automatically inherit the celestial kingdom.[800]

Interestingly, the Mormons do not believe that we begin with conception. According to their doctrines, we have always existed.[726]

BE KILLED BY A WILD ANIMAL
OR IN BATTLE

Although the Ob-Ugrian people are related to the Hungarians,[50] they live in Siberia and have typical Siberian shamans. These shamans use drums to go into a trance and they have animal spirits to help them journey to another world.[50]

The Ob-Ugrian believe that men who are killed by a wild animal or in a battle go straight to a sky world. The rest go to an underworld.[50, 397]

AS THE UNIVERSALISTS SAY, PERHAPS,
IN THE END, EVERYONE IS SAVED

As Helena Blavatsky, the celebrated theosophist leader, pointed out, Christians invented eternal damnation.[90] Before Christianity, the idea of eternal damnation existed in no other religion.[90] In CE 543, however, the Synod of Constantinople made this rule:

> If anyone shall say or think that there is a time limit to the torment of demons or ungodly persons, or that there will ever be an end to it, or that they will be pardoned or made whole again, let him be excommunicated.

A small number of Christians, however, have embraced the idea of Christian Universalism, the idea that everyone is ultimately saved.[132]

Origen, for example, appears to have been a universalist. Origen taught that hell was not forever, and all sinners, including Satan himself, will be embraced by god and will eventually join the communion of saints.[585, 300, 9, 132] These are the eloquent words of Origen:

> Since, as we have often pointed out, the soul is eternal and immortal, it is possible that, in vast and immeasurable spaces, throughout long and various ages, it can descend from the highest good to the lowest evil, or it can be restored from ultimate evil to the greatest good.[875]

Several scriptural texts seem to endorse universalism:

For as in Adam all die, so in Christ all will be made alive. (1 Corinthians 15:22)

And all mankind will see God's salvation. (Luke 3:6)

For this we labor and strive, that we have put our hope in the living God, who is the Savior of all men, and especially of those who believe. (1 Timothy 4:10)

And we have seen and testify that the Father has sent his Son to be the Savior of the world. (1 John 4:14)

But I, when I am lifted up from the earth, will draw all men to myself. (John 12:32)

Universalists are found in the modern world; one group, called the Primitive Baptist Universalists, is located primarily in the central Appalachian region of the United States.[239]

BECOME A WITCH

According to the great Gerald Gardner (1884–1964), Witchcraft, or Wicca, is an ancient tradition that was only revealed to the modern world in 1954.[328]

A nature religion, Wicca honors the horned god of the forest, who is "strong, virile, and loving," but the goddess figure, depicted as the virgin, the mother, and the wise old crone, has primacy.[419, 819, 327]

According to Gerald Gardner, witches believe that ordinary people go to an afterlife, where they gather with "like-minded people." It will be "pleasant or unpleasant" according to their natures. According to their merits, they may be reincarnated in time.[328]

Witches, on the other hand, go to a special place called Summerland, a place of rest and refreshment. In Summerland they will grow young again, until they are ready for reincarnation on earth.[328, 419, 526]

Just as Druze believe they are always reborn as Druze,[78] witches believe that witches are always reborn in witch's circles. And, over time, some of them may become demi-gods, known as the "Mighty Dead."[328]

Witches also believe—and this idea was especially dear to Gardner—that "if we perform the rites correctly, by the grace of the Great Mother we will be reborn among those we loved." [328, 419] In other words, love does not end with death, but brings the lover and beloved together again and again.

In the words of Gerald Gardner:

For there are three great events in the life of man—love, death, and resurrection in the new body—and magic controls them all. To fulfill love you must return again at the same time and place as the loved ones, and you must remember and love her or him again.[328]

HAVE THE CORRECT TATTOOS

As life slips away, the Sioux Indians ask to be taken outside, so that they can die under the open sky.[253] Like all American Indians, they sing a death-song, a personal chant. The dying Indian has rehearsed it his entire life. Guttural in tone, the song usually terrifies the outsiders who hear it.[922]

The Sioux believe that the Milky Way is the path followed by souls. As the dead travel to the otherworld, they will pass the campfires of the dead.[904]

Eventually, the dead meet an old woman, and she decides their fates. If they have the proper tattoos, she admits them to the otherworld, a happy place that is the land of many lodges.[382]

If the dead do not have the proper tattoos, however, she will push them over a cliff. They will fall back to earth, where they will become ghosts.[382]

Traditionally, like many warrior societies, a Sioux man believes that all the men he has killed in this world will be his slaves in the next world.[441]

PERFORM A VEDIC SACRIFICE

The Hindus believe that the Vedas—their holy texts—are not man-made. Uncreated and eternal, they have existed forever in the form of sound, only becoming known when they were heard by the ancient sages.[487, 536]

Veda means "knowing" or "knowledge." The most important of the Vedas, the *Rig Veda,* has 1028 hymns, 153,826 words, and 432,000 syllables.[825]

According to the *Purva Mimamsa,* a Hindu philosophical text, when a Hindu Vedic sacrifice is correctly performed, it produces an incorruptible substance called *apurva.*[487] Independent of the gods, this substance is at the sacrificer's disposal after death. Whatever else the sacrificer has done, if he has apurva from a sacrifice, *he can enter a heaven whether or not the gods are willing.*[487]

The greatest Hindu animal sacrifice is the Ashvamedha or "horse sacrifice." Kings perform this horse sacrifice before assuming universal power. This ritual is so powerful that the *Bhagavata Purana* states that the extermination of the whole human race could be atoned for by one Ashvamedha.[487, 513, 81]

The Ashvamedha is described in detail in the *Yajur Veda* (and in the commentary in the *Shatapatha Brahmana*).

Only a king could conduct an Ashvamedha. The horse that is sacrificed must be a stallion, older than twenty-four, but younger than one hundred years.[951]

WAIT FOR SAOSHYANT THE SAVIOR

According to tradition, the Iranian sage Zoroaster, who is also called Zarathustra, was a prophet who laughed when he was born.[261, 912] Not surprisingly, his religion has optimistic expectations.

Although Zoroastrianism has a hell, the abode of evil-doers, evil-thinkers, and evil-speakers, god, who is called Ahura Mazda (Wise Lord), visits the sinners in hell five days each year.[585, 47, 630]

Viewed as a ghastly pit that is crowded with the damned, each individual in hell thinks that he is alone.[459] The people there eat poison.[261]

Interestingly, the Zoroastrian "hell" has no fire. Fire is sacred in the Zoroastrian creed, so the wicked suffer from a lack of fire, and they endure bitter cold and darkness.[9, 261]

The Zoroastrian hell, however, is not eternal,[459] and it endures only until the "renovation" of the world.[9]

At the end of this universe, according to the Zoroastrians, a savior named Saoshyant will come from god. Then, the dead will be raised—the good and evil will be resurrected—and everyone will rise in the places where they died.[273]

A great "renovation" will occur, and all people will pass through molten metal. For the good, the hot metal will feel like warm milk; for the bad, the metal will feel like liquid fire.[9, 261]

All will be purified, and everyone will praise god. All will become immortal in glorified bodies. (Previously, in heaven and hell, individuals were spirits.)[9] Men and women will become forty years of age, and people who died as children will become fifteen.[9, 273, 630, 912]

At the end, Ahriman (the evil counter-god who is the source of all evil and death) will be rendered completely harmless by god.[261] The evil one's realm will be destroyed and all will live in paradise forever.[9]

ACCEPT ALLAH AND
MUHAMMAD AS HIS PROPHET

Islam is a product of the desert. The desert: vast, silent, and clean, like an empty cathedral.

Notably, from any perspective, the entire universe almost seems to be a type of desert, and the "stars are but thistles in that waste."[193]

Given its origins, Islam is a religion of extremes: paradise and damnation, good and evil, black and white. Like the desert itself, Islam is uncompromising. According to Muslim teaching, 99 percent of all humans are destined for hell.[235]

According to tradition, Muhammad (circa 570–632 CE), the "seal of the prophets," was born circumcised.[766, 333] The prophet received his calling on his "night of power."[766, 445 682]

Islam teaches that Jesus, a previous prophet, predicted the coming of Muhammad. In the Gospel of John 14:16, Jesus speaks these words: "And I will pray the Father, and he shall give you another Comforter, that he may abide with you forever."[121]

To become a Muslim is simple. According to Islam, anyone who recites a simple phrase—"There is no god but Allah, and Mohammad is his prophet"—becomes a Muslim.[766]

Islam clearly believes in an afterlife. In this religion, the dead die but they are re-created with memories.[865]

For believers, Muslims have a lavish paradise that contains beautiful virgins, water, wine, milk, fruits, and wealth. This heaven is for the faithful only.[506]

Although Islam is a Puritan religion, the faithful will be free to indulge in pleasure in the next world. Jalal al Din al Suyuti, an Egyptian commentator who lived between 1445–1505 CE, claimed that the believers will enjoy a permanent erection in paradise, and their penises will "never soften." They will each have seventy-two full-bosomed virgins—with dark eyes and desirable pudenda—and these women will be always willing and always compliant.[509]

These are the words of the Koran (Sura 78): "As for the righteous, they shall surely triumph. Theirs shall be gardens and vineyards, and high-bosomed virgins for companions: a truly overflowing cup."

For unbelievers, however, Islam teaches that their destination is hell. For eternity, infidels will hear the shrieks of the damned and they will smell the stink of charred flesh.

These are the words of the Koran (Sura 22):

Garments of fire have been prepared for the unbelievers. Scalding water shall be poured upon their heads, melting their skins and that which is in their bellies. They shall be lashed with rods of iron. Whenever, in their anguish, they try to escape from Hell, back they shall be dragged, and will be told: "Taste the torment of the Conflagration!"

Notably, Islam teaches that ALL Muslims will ultimately enjoy paradise. *Bad* Muslims will reside in hell temporarily, but they will go to heaven if there is "one atom of faith in their hearts."[291, 9, 766]

For Muslims, hell is only a place of purgation, from which they always emerge.[799, 9, 766]

BELIEVE JESUS IS THE CHRIST

The idea that to have religious faith is meritorious was not a classical Greek idea, so "to doubt" was not regarded as a crime, except where it interfered with public institutions.[825]

But, in Christian tradition, as in Islam, faith became the ultimate virtue. Martin Luther (1483–1546), the proponent of fundamentalist biblicism (that the Bible is the absolute word of God) and literalism (the idea that we must study the "plain sense" of the word when reading the Scriptures), thought that *no man deserved salvation.* Instead, men are saved by their faith that Jesus (6–4 BCE to 30–33 CE), a Jew from Galilee, is the Messiah who rose from the dead.[261]

In other words, salvation is a gift from God to those who believe.

According to Bible-based Christian fundamentalism, discussed by many Protestant theologians, including Jonathan Edwards (1703–1758) in his classic *Justification by Faith Alone,* there is only one way to Heaven: "Jesus saith unto him, I am the way, the truth, and the life: no man cometh unto the Father, but by me" (John 14:6).

Doing good deeds—practicing virtue—cannot save a soul: "For by grace are ye saved through faith; and that not of yourselves: it is the gift of God: Not of works, lest any man should boast" (Ephesians 2:8-9).

Only faith in Jesus, the reputed Messiah or Christ, can save a person from eternal damnation. Christ, claim the fundamentalists, died for the human race, was buried, and rose from the dead: "For God so loved the world, that he gave his only begotten Son, that whosoever believeth in him should not perish, but have everlasting life" (John 3:16).

This faith, like faith in Krishna or Amida Buddha in Asian religions, has great power: "That if thou shalt confess with thy mouth the Lord Jesus, and shalt believe in thine heart that God hath raised him from the dead, thou shalt be saved" (Romans 10:9).

And this salvation applies to the entire human race. In the words of Paul of Tarsus (circa 5–circa 67 CE): "For whosoever shall call upon the name of the Lord shall be saved" (Romans 10:13).

This faith must be absolute: "Though he slay me, yet will I trust him" (Job 13:15).

One paragon of the Christian tradition was David Livingstone (1813–1873), the famous Congregationalist missionary to Africa. Sick in the interior of Africa, when he sensed that death was coming, he made his final journal entry, prayed his last prayer, and, with his Bible open before him, he died on his knees.[861]

READ AND UNDERSTAND
THE SECRET GOSPEL OF THOMAS

The Gospel of Thomas, which was lost for innumerable centuries, was rediscovered in 1945 in Egypt.[587] Perhaps, as Tibetan holy men say about their termas, or treasures, scriptures are discovered when the human race is ready for them.[820]

Originally scholars argued that the work was written in the second century after Christ, but recent research suggests it was written in the first century. Indeed, recent research suggests that the Gospel of Thomas is older than the four orthodox gospels in the Bible.[474]

According to the Gospel of Thomas, which contains 114 sayings of Jesus, "These are the hidden words that the living Jesus spoke and Judas Thomas wrote them down."[347]

Judas Thomas refers to the twin brother of Jesus, the one called St. Thomas. In another work, the *Acts of Thomas,* Judas Thomas is called "twin of Christ, apostle of the Most High and fellow initiate into the hidden word of Christ, who receives his hidden sayings."[347, 101, 8, 238]

Jesus, in the Gospel of Thomas, makes this declaration: "Whoever finds the interpretation of these sayings will not experience death."

BE BORN A YEZIDI AND
HONOR THE PEACOCK ANGEL

The inscrutable Yezidis, who are mainly found in Nineveh Province in Iraq, are devoted to Melek Ta'us, which means the "Peacock King" or "Peacock Angel" in Kurdish.[16] Unlike the rest of the human race, the Yezidis claim they are descended from Adam alone. Since they consider themselves a chosen people, no one may join their religion. One must be born into the faith.[428]

The Peacock Angel, say the Yezidis, is master of this world. Prosperity and health as well as failure and sickness are in his power. Those who serve the Peacock Angel will prosper, but those who curse him will suffer.[274]

Melek Ta'us is very literally the rebel angel (the peacock is the symbol of pride). Although they deny that he is the devil, according to the *Black Scripture,* a 152-line sacred text, "None of us is allowed to utter his name, nor anything that resembles it, such as *Seitan* (Satan)."[428, 274] The Yezidis believe that they will be struck blind if they speak the forbidden name.[274]

The Yezidis believe that god created this universe, but now he is involved in this universe only one day each year. On that day—New Year's Day, the first Wednesday in April—god sits on his throne. On that day, say the Yezidis, no drums may be beaten,[428] and only funeral music is played.[274]

The Yezidis do not worship god, for he is passively benevolent and can only forgive. The Peacock Angel, however, is a powerful being who is actively malevolent, and the Yezidis believe it is prudent to propitiate him.[428, 274]

Their other sacred book, a distinctive work called the *Book of Revelation,* lays down no rules or commandments, but promises rewards to those who revere the Peacock Angel, and calamities to those who do not.[274]

These words are from the *Book of Revelation*: "I allow everyone to follow the dictates of his own nature, but he that opposes me will regret it sorely."[428]

Also from their *Book of Revelation*: "I am ever present to help all who trust in me and call upon me in times of need. There is no place in the universe that knows not my presence."[428]

The Yezidis never pray. The Peacock Angel is sufficiently powerful to save them without prayer.[274]

When a member of the Yezidi faith dies, they bury the corpse on the right side, with the head to the south.[274] They are interred with grave earth from the tomb of Sheikh Adi, a mysterious figure who died in 1162 CE.[274, 7]

The Yezidis believe in reincarnation, and their *Book of Revelation* declares that "if I so desire, I send a person a second or a third time into this world or into some other by the transmigration of souls."[428]

Because of their belief, some Yezidis hide silver and gold coins that they plan to retrieve if they are born a second time in this world.[428]

Is the Peacock Angel actually the devil? That is uncertain, but the Christian Bible, in II Corinthians 4:4, does call the devil "the god of this world."

UNDERSTAND THAT THE OTHERWORLD
WILL BE WHAT YOU EXPECT IT TO BE

We Experience What We Believe

According to nondualist thought (called idealism in the West), everything is a product of mind. To use the eloquent words of Professor Zimmer, "There is no thinker, there is only thought."[963]

Although we experience the events, the sensations, and our own bodies as "objectively" real, if the nondualists are correct, THIS world, as the *Yoga Vasistha* affirms, is as real—or as unreal—as the pleasure of a sexual dream.[954]

Likewise, if the otherworld is *also* like a thought or a dream, the otherworld may simply be what we expect it to be. Like any dream, it would be self-created, and we would experience the events, the sensations, and our own dream bodies as "objectively" real. And, like a dream, the imagination would perform the function of sense organs, and the imagination would provide objects to engage our "thought-attention."[699, 787]

Now, if the next world is literally a product of beliefs, expectations, and preconceptions, an idea endorsed by the *Yoga Vasistha* (and modern writers such by H. H. Price, John Hick, and Yogi Ramacharaka),[699, 391, 710] then—very literally—the Odinist will find his fabled Valhalla, the Christian will find his joyous Heaven, the Plains Indian will find bison and wild cherry juice in his "Happy Hunting Ground," and the Muslim will find his seventy-two buxom virgins.[70] As for the "convinced materialist," after death he would experience the "total emptiness" that he expects.[429] Since the materialist would remain "psychically" conscious, he would perhaps believe that he is languishing in some protracted nightmare.

To explain this concept, the *Yoga Vasistha* tells the interesting story of Queen Lila. When her husband dies, the queen asks Sarasvati, the goddess of wisdom, to reveal the secret of the next world. Lila wants to know where her husband is and what he is experiencing.

Granting the wish, the goddess of wisdom puts Lila's mind into her husband's consciousness. Although he has passed away, Lila learns that he does not realize that he is dead and he thinks that he is still living with his beloved wife at his side.[954]

Lila is confused, but the goddess explains that we create our own after-death state based on expectations and desires. In the afterlife, her husband's mind has projected a replica of the world that he left, exact in every detail.[954, 442]

VII

Ghosts and Specters

When the Dead Are Here

Men of light worship the gods of Light; men of Fire worship the gods of power and wealth; men of darkness worship ghosts and the spirits of the night.

BHAGAVAD GITA

Millions of spiritual creatures walk the earth
Unseen, both when we wake, and when we sleep.

JOHN MILTON, *PARADISE LOST*

Do not resort to ghosts and spirits, nor make yourself unclean by seeking them out.

LEVITICUS 19:31

The Thompson River Indians in British Columbia, wrote scholar James Teit, believe that "the soul of a person who has a nightmare is nearing the beginning of the trail heading to the world of souls."[415] In other words, our free soul or dream soul has traveled to the edge of the otherworld.

Sometimes, however, we can perhaps see the dead here—in our world—when we are fully awake.

This chapter deals with ghosts and specters. When studying the material, always remember Professor Erwin Rohde's warning that humans should never look directly at otherworldly beings or gods.[738]

WHAT IS A GHOST?

A pale opacity that is sometimes translucent, a ghost, as indicated above, is a "manifestation of the dead before the living."[212] In English, the word *ghost* originally meant a "visitor" or "guest."[26]

We have never found a culture that does not believe in the existence of ghosts,[312, 585] and ghost sightings still are common. It is said that England alone has 50,000 specters,[212] with York being the most haunted city in Europe.[212] Pluckley, in Kent, is England's most haunted village.[212]

Interestingly, the Greek word *theos,* which means "god," derives from a root designating "soul" or "spirit of the deceased," and the idea of god may have developed from the "deified dead."[261, 50] In effect, "god" may have begun as a "ghost."

TYPES OF CONTACT

Although *most* apparitions of the dead appear within one hour of death,[71] some may be seen in this world for years.

In the case of the so-called "wraith" or "crisis apparition,"[729] which appears right after death, it is usually to those who know the person, and the ghost is trying to convey a message. This may be a farewell, words of support, information on the location of an important document, or evidence of a crime.[305, 300]

In the second case, which is also called a "haunting," the viewers usually do not know the entity, whose actions are repetitive and often seem purposeless.[305, 300]

One noted wraith was the poet Dante Alighieri (circa 1265–1321). After Dante's death, thirteen cantos of his masterpiece, the *Divine Comedy,* were missing and presumed lost. Interestingly, Dante's wraith allegedly appeared to his son Jacopo and told him that the cantos were hidden in a wall. Jacopo found the manuscript, covered in mildew, in the location described by the wraith.[85, 729]

Another wraith was Marsilio Ficino (1433–1499), the humanist philosopher. He had made a "death pact" with Michel Mercanti, another philosopher. They promised to each other that the first of them to die would return to describe life beyond the grave. According to Mercanti, Ficino appeared at the hour of his death.[65]

The Marquis of Rambouillet and the Marquis of Précy made a similar pact in the time of Louis XIV. Following his death in Flanders, Rambouillet appeared the next day to his friend in Paris.[65]

The second type of manifestation—long-term hauntings—tend to conform to a pattern. The same sequence of events—such as a woman descending a stairwell—is seen repeatedly.[305]

Count Eberhard, who lived in the fifteenth century, saw a recurring manifestation, a ghost that had been condemned to hunt the same stag until "judgment day." The specter had been pursuing his quarry for five centuries when he was seen by Eberhard. Revolting in appearance, the phantom hunter had a face the size of a fist that was wrinkled like a leaf.[519]

Another long-term haunting is associated with Forde House, in England. Here, according to the legend, a girl was forced into a nunnery so that she would not make an unsuitable marriage, but she escaped with her lover's help. Her father, filled with wrath, hunted them down, killed the man, and then walled his own daughter alive in a wall in his home. Allegedly, there is still a ghost there today.[122]

A third long-term haunting involves Gertrude of Orlamunde, the infamous "White Lady." A fourteenth-century mistress of a Hohenzollern prince, Gertrude gouged out her children's eyes and murdered them when the prince refused to marry her. She later committed suicide in prison.[608]

When the specter of the "White Lady" is seen, disaster follows for the ancient Hohenzollern family.[608]

Kaiser Wilhelm II (1859–1941), the last Hohenzollern leader of Germany, reputedly saw her on August 31, 1914.[608]

DIFFERENT IDEAS ABOUT GHOSTS

Although every culture believes in ghosts, ideas about them differ.

According to the ancient Mesopotamians—who created one of the first civilizations—when the flesh perishes, two entities remain: bones and ghost. *Etemmu*—an Akkadian word—means "ghost." The word does not mean a spirit or a soul because—according to Mesopotamian religion—living humans do *not* have one.[637] If bones are not properly buried, the ghost haunts and walks in our world.[637] The specter, in other words, is one of the restless dead.

In ancient Greece, the unburied dead also could not enter the otherworld and they became ghosts. Thus, to punish executed criminals and to deprive them of peace, the Greeks threw them unburied into a pit.[637] In his *Laws,* Plato recommends denial of burial for sacrilege, the murder of a family member, and other serious crimes.[689, 111]

According to the Maricopa Indians of the American Southwest, however, a "ghost is just the shadow of a dead person."[415]

Likewise, according to the Lillooet Indians of North America, "ghosts are the shadows of souls." Just as every living body casts its shadow on the earth, so every soul has its ghost.[415]

Among the Choctaw Indians of North America, the specter is one of our souls that remains behind after death. The Choctaw say that we have two souls: the outside shadow, which always follows us, and the inside shadow, which at death goes to the otherworld. After death, the outside shadow stays here and becomes a grave ghost.[415]

The Ojibway Indians (Chippewa), on Parry Island in Canada, say that we have three parts: the body, the soul, and the shadow. The body decays at death, the soul journeys to the otherworld in the west, and the shadow becomes the grave ghost.[415]

The Chinese say we have two souls. The superior soul is the *hun* soul, called the "cloud daemon." The family calls it back to inhabit a special ancestral stone tablet in the house. There is one for every dead father, grandfather, great-grandfather (their wives' names appear on these tablets or the wives have their own stone slabs).[9, 273, 92, 535]

The family makes offerings to the hun and communicates with it. When something happens in the family, such as birth, death, marriage, and even a job promotion, it is announced to the ancestors with offerings.[9, 139, 637, 207]

The other soul is the *p'o* soul. Called the "white daemon," it will reside in the grave for at least three years, after which it will go to a netherworld called Yellow Springs. (Yellow symbolizes the soil.) If it becomes angry, disturbed, or is maltreated while still on earth, the white daemon could become a ghost. It will eventually disintegrate.[637, 207]

To discourage leakage of the p'o soul or the entrance of foreign souls seeking a human, the Chinese seal all the apertures of the corpse. They also use watertight coffins and elixirs to prevent or slow the decay of the body.[637]

According to Paracelsus (1493–1541), the European Renaissance scholar, man has three components: the body, the soul, and "a middle substance, betwixt the soul and the body."[212]

This "middle substance" hovers around the dead body. A kind of "astral spirit" or "astral corpse," it consists of matter, but it takes longer to decompose than the body. It preserves the thoughts, desires, and imaginations that were impressed upon the mind at the time of death.[212]

Thus, the murder victim's astral spirit would convey the horror connected to his murder—especially if he died in an especially gruesome manner.[212]

Finally, Frederic W. H. Myers (1843–1901), a Victorian researcher and a founder of the Society for Psychical Research, believed that ghosts are "projections generated by the incoherent dreams of the dead."[212] In other words, some telepathic communication may exist between the spiritual and the material world, and when we see a ghost, we may be seeing *a dead person's dream.*[212, 611]

The theory of Myers would explain "hauntings" in which the same specter is seen doing the same thing repeatedly. In effect, we are seeing a dead person's recurring nightmare.

APPEARANCE OF GHOSTS

Plato said that we can see ghosts because they were wicked people in life. Good souls are transparent, but evil souls are visible.[690, 35, 540]

Some people have seen semi-transparent apparitions,[305] but they may be old specters that are fading away.

Contrary to popular belief, ghosts appear to be three-dimensional,[305] and they follow the laws of perspective and parallax.[71]

Although they sometimes seem to glide rather than walk,[305] they will open doors and walk around furniture.[305] Their movements will conform to the "domestic geography" of *their* past, however, so they may pass through our walls if those walls did not exist in their lifetimes.[305]

In York, England, for example, people can see Roman soldiers marching by that are visible from the waist up only, for the soldiers are marching on the old Roman road of Eboricum. That Roman road lies a few feet lower than the road level of modern York.[35]

Although ghosts resemble the living, Plutarch (circa 46–120 CE) said the souls of the dead can be recognized by the absence of their shadow and their unblinking eyes.[112]

Otherwise, however, the ghost has the appearance that he had at the moment of death. Plato said that the soul retains the scars of its former existence.[111, 688]

Virtually all ghosts are clothed, and naked ghosts are rare.[212] Typically, the ghost wears the clothing that he wore in his final hours.[519]

Until the nineteenth century, the poor—who were buried without coffins—were inhumed in winding sheets or shrouds of linen, and they were otherwise naked.[519, 702, 212] As a result, exceptionally old ghosts may appear in sheets or shrouds.

If ghosts are wearing clothing, of what is it made?

There have been phantom ships, coaches, and cars, as Eugene Crowell points out in *Spirit World: Its Inhabitants, Nature, and Philosophy*,[190] so that could explain the other inanimate objects associated with specters, such as their clothing and shoes.[212] In other words, perhaps such objects are not as inanimate as we think.

WHERE TO FIND GHOSTS

Everywhere in the world, disembodied spirits haunt crossroads.[313] Not surprisingly, Hecate, the Greek goddess of ghosts and sorcery, often visited crossroads, especially where three roads come together.[130, 706, 243, 444]

Ghosts are also drawn to empty houses. In earlier times, houses were not left vacant for more than two weeks because ghosts could infest the homes.[212]

In Europe, some old great houses have windowless rooms where, before modern psychology, wealthy families confined lunatics in the family.[122] Such houses, especially when vacant, would be prime locations for hauntings.[122]

A common belief is that the doorway is a gathering place for ghosts. Since the threshold belongs neither to the inside world nor to the outside world, it is a supernaturally endowed space.[444]

A great deal of haunting occurs around water, such as a stream or a river, or a lake. When ghosts are seen in marshy places, they are sometimes called "will-o-the-wisps."[212]

According to an old belief, found from Europe to Aboriginal Australia, the dead cannot cross water—if they are compelled to attempt it, they will melt into thin air—so they gather on the shores adjacent to water.[122, 915]

Water, moreover, is a border between this world and the otherworld.[519] Like a scrying mirror (a reflective surface used to contact the dead), it is a portal between the living and dead.[212]

Specters are also found where there are unburied dead. Thus, the Smithsonian Institution in the United States, which contains the bones of at least 33,000 humans,[427] should contain specters.

Finally, ghosts will be found where crimes or atrocities have occurred. According to Guido von List (1848–1919), an act of violence impregnates the place where it is committed.[772, 924]

For violence, consider the Coliseum in Rome. Covering six acres, with 48,440 square feet of arena space, at least 500,000 people died violent deaths there.[403, 923] That is approximately ten human deaths for every square foot of arena.

Another area soaked with human gore is the Tarawa Atoll, in the Pacific Ocean. The site of a savage battle in World War II that lasted seventy-six hours, at least 6,000 human lives were squandered in 300 acres of space (the size of the Pentagon and its parking lots).[18]

WHEN TO SEE GHOSTS

Night is the preferred time for ghosts. According to the *Eyrbyggja Saga,* which describes a haunting infestation, "No one could stay outside in peace, once the sun had set."[519] And one medieval ghost, when asked why he appeared at night, made this declaration: "As long as I cannot go to God, I remain in the night."[212]

Ghosts can be seen occasionally in the light of day, but all light, both natural and artificial, weakens them.[519] According to the *Poetic Edda,* "these enemies" called ghosts "are much more powerful at night than when the light of day dawns."[519, 697, 9]

According to Professor Claude Lecouteux, ghosts tend to manifest in winter, are most numerous around the winter solstice, when the nights are longest, and they become less common in spring, although they do not entirely disappear.[519]

The occurrence of bad weather is also important, and there seems to be a link between ghosts and storms.[519]

GHOSTS AND BURIED TREASURE

In traditional England, if someone sees a ghost, he should start digging at daylight, looking for gold coins or Roman treasure. According to Ella Leather, a folklorist, if someone hid or buried money or treasure, their ghost would haunt the spot.[212] An *Essay on the History and Reality of Apparitions,* by Daniel Defoe (circa 1660–1731), refers to the belief.[212, 228]

HOW TO MAKE A HOUSE HAUNTED

To make a house haunted, there is a voodoo spell from Haiti.

When a person dies in a house, a sorcerer secretly drives two nails into a beam in a house where the death took place. The dead person will be trapped in the house, and he will torment the family that lives there.[584]

To check if the technique has worked, light a candle. According to tradition, flames burn blue in the presence of specters. This is mentioned in Shakespeare's *Richard III.*[212, 780]

A HELPER GHOST

The fierce Inuit—slayers of men and eaters of meat who inhabit the harsh world of the Arctic—traditionally believed that a soul of a dead child empowered a hunter. The soul could be from an stillborn infant or a murdered baby. If murder is involved, the act must be kept secret.[313]

The hunter dries the little corpse and keeps it in a bag. When carried, it will help him find game and will assist his aim.[313]

SPEAKING TO GHOSTS

Ghosts are usually mute, and one study found that only 14 percent of specters speak.[212] When they do speak, it is in a hoarse tone and in a low voice.[212, 111]

According to Francis Grose, an eighteenth-century antiquarian, "a ghost has not the power to speak until he has been first spoken to."[212] And, once the specter speaks, it is dangerous to interrupt it or ask questions.[212]

According to the Japanese, the ghosts of old people are more reserved because they left the world with less resentment. Child ghosts, in contrast, are talkative.[86]

Always, when addressing a ghost, ask if there is anything that he wants.[86]

A GHOST IN THE FLESH

The Melanesian people in the Pacific believe that sharks are the abode of ghosts. Some men, before death, announce that they will become sharks. Such men are buried at sea. (People buried on land become land ghosts.)[312]

DANGEROUS GHOSTS

Angry ghosts—dangerous ghosts—have a stagnant and unpleasant smell,[86] so they are easily recognized. (In contrast, beneficent entities have a pleasant smell.)[212]

There are many dangerous ghosts—in Fiji, the most feared ghosts are "slain men, unchaste women, and women who died in childbed"[312, 72]—but perhaps the most infamous dangerous specters are the crew of the fabled ghost ship, the *Flying Dutchman*.[915, 24, 608] Reputedly sailing for eternity with a crew of dead souls (condemned for a terrible crime), the captain comes ashore every century to find a woman. According to legend, anyone who sees the *Flying Dutchman* will die a terrible death.[196]

An officer of HMS *Bacchante* allegedly saw the ship on July 11, 1881, and he described it as a phantom ship that glowed with a red light.[196] Soon after, the officer fell from the mast to his death.[196]

PROTECTION FROM GHOSTS

To protect yourself from specters, never mention the dead by name until his body is decayed and his bones are clean. By naming him, you summon him.[312]

Remember that it is dangerous to whistle in the dark. Whistling in the dark attracts spirits.[312]

Also, never venture out alone. According to the Aboriginal people of Australia, when a man is alone, a spirit, even of a loved one, may harm him, but a spirit will not molest people in a group.[312]

If you must venture into a haunted area, carry sharp or pointed objects, like knives or thorns. In many cultures, such things repel spirits.[300]

To be safe, travel with a dog, especially a spayed female. The writings of John Aubrey, a seventeenth-century writer, describe how in 1686 a man in Dorset, England, purged a haunted house with a "neutered bitch."[122]

If you see a specter, throw a handful of graveyard earth into his face. According to legend, this will make the ghost docile, and he will obey you.[122] John Evelyn (1620–1706), the English diarist, said that the most potent grave earth is from St. Innocent's Church in Paris, but that church no longer exists.[122]

For added security, draw a circle on the ground around yourself. In many traditions, the ghost cannot break the circle.[519, 122]

LAYING A GHOST

To lay a ghost—to stop him from harassing the living—find his corpse. In most traditions, the ghost will stay near his body, especially in cases of violent or premature death, including suicide.[300]

After locating his cadaver, dismember it, crush the skull, stake it to the earth, cremate it, submerge it under water with weights, or bury it face down.[212]

Sometimes, multiple methods are used. In London, in 1834, Nicholas Steinberg, a murderer who committed suicide, was presumed to be too evil to rest in peace, so his skull was smashed and he was buried face down in his grave. This was to keep him from haunting.[214]

PROTECTION FOR MURDERERS

To prevent their slain enemies from returning, the early Finnish people ate the hearts and livers of the persons they had killed. (By doing so, the killer also gained the dead man's strength.)[50]

In ancient Greece, murderers practiced *maschalismos,* or mutilation of the murder victim's corpse. The mutilation rendered the dead person harmless and prevented him from harassing or harming his killer.[444, 330]

READING DOWN A GHOST

"Reading Down a Ghost" is a Christian method to render a specter harmless.

A group of clergymen must assemble in a church. Standing in a circle, each holding a candle, they must together read the psalms over and over throughout the night. Eventually, the candles will grow dimmer, and they will go out one by one. When only one candle is left burning, the man holding it will be the most powerful and learned one present.[122]

When one candle remains, the ghost shrinks in size. He will become so small that he can be stuffed into a little box or bottle, and that can be disposed of in a pool of water or some isolated place. At Bagley, in Dorset, England, the specter of an old squire is imprisoned in a chimney.[122]

VIII

Communicating
with the Dead

From Necromancy to Scrying

*I shall not commit the fashionable stupidity of regarding
everything I cannot explain as a fraud.*
CARL GUSTAV JUNG, "THE PSYCHOLOGICAL
FOUNDATIONS OF BELIEF IN SPIRITS"

But how can we be dead? We are just as we were before.
A PILOT KILLED WITH HIS CREW IN WORLD WAR II,
TO AIR CHIEF MARSHAL LORD DOWDING,
AT A SÉANCE

*Any man or woman among you who calls up ghosts or
spirits shall be put to death.*
LEVITICUS 20:27

*The wakeful man trying to remember his dreams is like
a dead man trying to gather together his memories of life.*
JEAN BAUDRILLARD, *FRAGMENTS:
COOL MEMORIES III, 1990–1995*

Arthur Balfour, the first Earl of Balfour and the prime minister of the United Kingdom between 1902 and 1905, deeply loved Mary Catherine Lyttleton. Before they could announce their engagement, however, she died of typhus on Palm Sunday, March 21, 1875.

Heartbroken, Balfour remained a bachelor for the rest of his life. According to the late Professor Fontana, a psychologist and parapsychologist, Balfour tried to communicate with his lost love over the years, especially every Palm Sunday, which Balfour always spent with Lyttleton's sister, her sister's husband, and a bishop.[305]

It is unclear if Balfour succeeded, but this section contains techniques he could have used.

KEEP TWO WARNINGS IN MIND

When communicating with the dead, always remember the warning of celebrated British author Colin Wilson (1931–2013) that spirits often lie.[936] In particular, the "ordinary dead" may lie to glamorize themselves.[305]

Also, always remember that communicating with the dead can be hazardous.

In January 1949, a young boy was given a Ouija board by his dying aunt so that he could talk to her. The boy, who was fourteen years old, was named Douglas Deen, and a few weeks after his aunt passed away, he allegedly became possessed. The story, which was reported in the *Washington Post* on August 20, 1949, would later become the inspiration for William Peter Blatty's celebrated horror novel, *The Exorcist*.[417, 183, 563]

ARE THE COMMUNICATIONS REAL?

If contact is established, we can never be certain who or what is talking to us.

One curious case is known as the Philip Experiment. It is unclear if the séance team was contacting a real entity, a lying spirit, or a *tulpa* (a "thought form" brought into being by the minds of the people involved[208]).

For the Philip Experiment, conducted in Canada in 1972, the

Toronto Society of Psychical Research intentionally created a *fictional* person from seventeenth-century England. In their fabricated biography, he supposedly committed suicide after his "gypsy lover" had been burned as a witch.[305]

Strangely, in 1973, "he" began to communicate. Initially, the details of the communications coincided with the imaginary biography, but "he" began to develop mischievous traits and to work spectacular effects, such as a table chasing people without being touched, and lights going on and off.[48]

WHAT DO THE DEAD KNOW?

Scientists suggest that the human mind can store approximately 10^{15} bits of information. That corresponds to approximately 1,000 years of "subjective" life.[865]

But, that is the mind of a living human. What about the mind of the dead?

According to the ancient Greeks, a living human changes constantly, but the "psyche" of the dead is changeless. To us the words of Professor Eva C. Keuls, "the psyche of the dead is frozen in time at the moment of death, in appearance as well as experience."[330]

In other words, if a living man communicates with someone who died fifty years ago, the deceased would know only what he knew when he died.

The Jewish scholar, Levi ben Gershom, also known as Gersonides (1288–1344), agreed. For Gersonides, study and intellectual attainment while alive are important because once we are dead, we do not continue to grow and evolve, but enjoy only the knowledge that we accumulated in life.[716]

Given the limited knowledge of the dead, the ancient Greeks consulted an ordinary ghost to gain information on the past—or to use his wisdom—but not to gain information on the present or the future.[300]

If the seeker of knowledge wants to know the future, he summons a dead *prophet*. Thus, Odysseus summoned the dead seer named

Teiresias,[401, 50, 273] the Witch of Endor summoned the dead prophet Samuel,[83] Odin, in a necromantic ceremony in the *Eddaic Verses,* summoned a dead seeress with a "corpse-reviving spell."[697, 433, 519, 831, 261]

TRY ONE OF TWO TYPES OF NECROMANCY

Necromancy is communication with the dead. Because the necromancer may unintentionally summon a malicious spirit, the procedure always carries risks.[212]

According to Heinrich Cornelius Agrippa von Nettesheim (1486–1535), a Renaissance occultist, there were two types of necromancy.[11, 212] The first is traditional necromancy, or raising the bodies of the dead.[212] An ancient practice, the technique required sacrificial blood.[212] According to Porphyry (circa 234–circa 305 CE), souls prefer freshly spilt blood, which seems (for a short time) to restore to them some of the faculties of life.[90]

The second type is sciomancy. Here, the necromancer calls and communicates with a spirit only. When medieval sorcerers tried to summon Judas Iscariot,[211] they used sciomancy. Also, the modern séance is a type of sciomancy.

Whatever method used, Agrippa said the dead are "not easily raised up," except for the extremely wicked, those who have died from violence, and those who are unburied.[11, 212]

Moreover, according to Ebenezer Sibly, an eighteenth-century occultist, only the spirits of those murdered in "circumstances uncommonly horrid and execrable" were able to speak.[212]

Two Necromantic Ceremonies in Literature

Lucan (39–65 CE), the Roman writer, describes a necromantic procedure in *Pharsalia*. In this classic account, Sextus Pompey asks the Thessalian witch Erichtho to see the future. Using a freshly deceased body, she drags it to a cave with a metal hook. Covering herself with her robe and placing a viper on her brow, she uses the saliva of a mad dog, the entrails of a lynx, the marrow of stags fed only on serpents, the backbone of a corpse-fed hyena, and other loathsome ingredients. Barking like a dog and howling like a wolf, she summons the soul with her chants. At first it refuses to enter the corpse, but she threatens the soul, and she also promises to burn his body when she is finished, thereby insuring that the deceased would never be disturbed again. Finally relenting, the ghost enters the cold corpse and answers questions.[341, 539]

In Homer's *Odyssey,* in another famous description of necromancy in literature, Circe tells Odysseus how to summon the dead. After digging a grave at the end of the world, he must make a threefold offering (milk and honey mixed, then wine and water, and over this white meal is sprinkled). He must make a prayer to Hades and Persephone, the king and queen of the underworld. He must slaughter a black ram and a black sheep and cause their blood to flow into the pit. Souls will gather to drink the warm blood and they will briefly awaken to consciousness. Afterward, to close the procedure, he must burn the sheep and the ram next to the pit.[130, 401, 738]

One Real Necromantic Ceremony

This procedure to awaken the dead is paraphrased from *Raising Hell: A Concise History of the Black Arts and Those Who Dared to Practice Them* by Robert Masello:

> Prepare yourself for nine days and nine nights. Wear grave clothes stolen from corpses. Recite a funeral service over yourself. Live on a diet of dog's flesh and black bread baked without salt or leavening. Drink the unfermented juice of grapes.
>
> After nine days, at midnight go to a grave. A stormy night—with wind, rain, and lightning—is best. It is difficult for the dead to communicate on a calm night.
>
> Draw a circle around the grave. Burn henbane, aloe wood, hemlock, saffron, opium, and mandrake. Open the grave and remove the corpse. Place the head of the cadaver to the east and the arms and legs in the position of "Christ crucified."

Ring a necromancy bell. This is a bell that has rested on a grave for seven days and seven nights. Such a bell has the power to awaken the dead.

Touch the corpse three times with a wooden wand and command it to rise. Three times command the corpse to answer questions. Declare to the corpse that it will wander and suffer torments for twenty-one years if it does not obey.

The corpse will sit up and answer all questions. The recently dead will answer in a hollow voice. Older cadavers will squeak incoherently.

When the rite is completed, reward the deceased by burning his corpse. A cremated cadaver can never be disturbed again.[562]

USE THE TALKING BOARD

The talking board, also called the Ouija board, is widely used today, often with stunning results.

In 1910, for example, the Ouija board informed Francisco Madero (1873–1913), who was interested in the Spiritism of the French writer Allan Kardec (1804–1869), that if he led a revolt, he would be the next leader of Mexico. As predicted, Madero indeed overthrew President Porfirio Diaz, and was elected president in 1911. Madero was assassinated in 1913, however (a fact that the board had neglected to reveal).[417]

The talking board is quite ancient.

Ammianus Marcellinus (330–395 CE), in the Roman Empire, described a table cut from a slab of stone. The letters of the alphabet were engraved on the slab. Marcellinus held a cord, with metal ring at bottom, above the slab table. As questions were posed, the ring swung a little to indicate the reply.[183, 528, 48]

Centuries later, in 1853 in France, Spiritualists began to use a small heart-shaped platform that rested on three legs, one of which was a pencil. When the platform moved, it wrote messages on paper.[417]

Elijah Bond (1847–1921), working with others, constructed the modern Ouija board in 1890.[417] The modern board contains numbers, letters, and the words *yes* and *no*.[526] In the modern Ouija, the planchette, which serves as a portal and is touched by hands, has a triangular symbol. According to legend, spirits often lie, but a spirit in a triangle must speak the truth.[788, 223, 936]

Practitioners claim that using the Ouija board may be hazardous. If the planchette repeatedly makes the figure eight—or goes from one corner to the next, hitting all four—an evil spirit is reputedly present.[183, 417]

If a silver coin is placed on the board at the start of the procedure, however, no evil spirit can come through.[183]

To discard a Ouija board, break it into seven pieces and bury it.[183] The board must not be burned, for anyone hearing a scream during the incineration will be dead within thirty-six hours.[183]

CONSULT AN ITAKO, A BLIND FEMALE MEDIUM IN JAPAN

An *itako* or *ichiko* is a blind female medium from Japan. They are found in the northeast part of the main island.[86]

According to legend, Northern Japan is a place where the dead and the living can meet. The area around Mount Osori—and the lake in its crater—is an eerie place. Treeless, there are jagged rocks and hot brimstone springs. Some of these springs, which smell like rotten eggs, are blood red, and some are yellow.[743]

People go to Mount Osori to consult shamans. Traditionally, these shamans, which are more like mediums, are blind women, and the older they are, the more powerful they are.[86]

A female can become an itako if she is born blind or becomes blind as a baby. (Seeing nothing in the light of day, they can see the invisible world.)[86] Studying under a teacher, an older itako, the young girl must undergo difficult ordeals first. Most start the process before menstruation.[86]

One initiation, described by Carmen Blacker in *The Catalpa Bow: A Study of Shamanistic Practices in Japan,* took place in 1935, and lasted 100 days. The girl subjected herself to harsh austerities, which included sleeplessness, semi-starvation, and extreme cold.[86]

The actual initiation is the climax of the ordeal, and it takes place in a dark room with members of her family and older mediums present.[86]

The older mediums form a circle around her and chant religious sutras. The young girl will feel the *kami*—the Shinto divine beings—enter the room, and one will possess her. The possession will cause her to pass out.[86]

When she awakens, she is now the wife of a *kami* (a god). Her teacher will dress her in white and there will be a wedding feast.[86]

She can now summon dead people (and the kami) and deliver messages to the people.[86]

CONDUCT A VISION QUEST

As Professor Denise Lardner Carmody points out in *The Oldest God: Archaic Religion Yesterday and Today,* most archaic people equate the real with the "vividly experienced." A dream, a vision, or a poetic image could be as real as the weapon in a man's hand.[147]

On the Great Plains of America, Indian warriors and hunters actively sought the assistance of spirits through vision quests and dreams. Virtually all North American Indians emphasized the *direct* experience of the spiritual.[415] Indians believe they must see or feel supernatural beings.[877]

Without this contact with the supernatural, for example, the Comanche warrior "believed he would walk helplessly through the world like a menstruating woman."[293]

These vision quests involved "ascetic preparations," such as prolonged fasts, absolute chastity, and painful flagellations. In particular, fasting is helpful: starvation weakens the flesh so that the spirit may dominate.[22]

The vision quests also required absolute solitude. In the words of one Native American sage, "The only true wisdom lives far from mankind, out in the great loneliness, and it can be reached only through suffering. Privation and suffering alone can open the mind of a man to all that is hidden in others."[441]

This is the technique used by Sioux warriors:[441]

Wear only a robe, a loincloth, and moccasins. Take only a knife, a pipe, and smoking materials.

Go to a high place where there is solitude. Remove every living thing from an area large enough to sit on or lie on.

As you enter your prepared space, ask the four winds not to bring inclement weather.

Once you have entered your prepared space, stay there until you have a vision or until you become convinced that you have failed. In the space, meditate on your quest.

You may invoke spirits, mentally or verbally, either in song or in prayer.

You may stand, sit, or lie down. You may be awake or asleep. But you must not leave the space.

You may smoke the tobacco pipe as often as you wish, but you must not eat or drink anything.

The vision may come when you are awake or asleep. It may appear as any living thing or any inanimate object.

It may be psychic in nature, or it could be a falling star, a sudden storm, a high wind, or a wolf call.

It may speak clearly, it may speak in a mysterious language that you do not understand, or it may speak in the language of birds or beasts.

Always, the vision will say or do something to confirm that it is the vision that you seek.

CONSULT A SCRYING DEVICE

The ancient Greeks consulted a celebrated oracle of the dead at Ephyra, in Epirus. Both Herodotus (circa 484–425 BCE) and Strabo (64/63 BCE–circa CE 24) discuss it in their writings.[598, 828, 389]

Sotoris Dakarisa, a Greek archaeologist, discovered the site in the 1950s.[598] Sotoris found an underground complex of passages and chambers leading to a huge bronze cauldron. Since he was a scientific nihilist, Sotoris suggested that priests concealed themselves in the cauldron and fabricated the voices![598]

Dr. Raymond Moody, who pioneered research into the "near-death experience," suggests in his writings that the ancients filled the polished bronze cauldron with water to create a "scrying" device. By staring into the reflective surface, people believed that they could make contact with the dead.[598]

Scrying devices have been used for paranormal visions for centuries. John Dee (1527–1608 or 1609), the mathematician and occultist who spied for the government of England (under agent code 007), reputedly used an obsidian divination mirror of the Aztecs (which the Spanish had stolen) to see spirits, including a female named Madimi. Interestingly, when Madimi manifested, she was able to walk around the house.[598]

Dr. Raymond Moody has constructed a modern scrying device that he calls the "Theatre of the Mind." Its components are so simple that anyone may reproduce it anywhere.[598]

Moody's apparition chamber has a mirror that is four feet high and three and one-half feet wide. A chair is placed three feet from the mirror, and the chair is inclined backward so that the gazer will see a "crystal-clear pool of darkness" instead of his own reflection. A curtain surrounds the chair and mirror, and behind the chair and inside the curtain is a candle or a "small stained-glass lamp with a fifteen-watt bulb."[598]

Moody instructs the gazer to bring mementos of the loved one they are trying to contact.[598] According to George Gurdjieff (circa 1877–1949), objects once possessed by the dead retain traces of the dead.[937]

Sessions start at dusk, and people may stay in as long as they wish. No clocks or mechanical timepieces are allowed, but an hourglass is permissible.[598]

Gazers are told to look into the mirror without trying to see anything. When visions begin, they must not try to direct them, but should just let them flow. In the beginning, attempting to ask direct questions will make the images fade away, so the gazer should simply have brief questions in his mind before he starts.[598]

Initially, the visions will last about ten minutes. With experience, however, the visions will last longer.[598]

Although seeing the dead is the goal, some contacts may be auditory only. Or, in some cases, the gazer may feel the apparition touch him.[598]

Using the device, Moody carried on a conversation with his own deceased grandmother. When he saw her, she seemed younger.[598]

She appeared solid, but she would not let him touch her. She appeared to be surrounded by light.[598]

They talked, but also seemed to know each other's thoughts.[598]

Other individuals have also used Moody's "theatre of the mind," and the reported results are interesting:[598]

- One-half of the gazers carried on conversations with apparitions.
- One-fourth saw a different deceased relative than the one they intended.
- One-tenth of the apparitions seemed to come out of the mirror.
- Some people said they were touched by an apparition.
- One-tenth of the gazers said they took journeys into the mirror.
- One-fourth reported seeing apparitions *only* after they left the theatre of the mind. If an off-site encounter occurred, it was usually within twenty-four hours.

USE TECHNOLOGY OR INSTRUMENTAL TRANSCOMMUNICATION

Technology and the paranormal seem to be strangely connected. When Waldemar Borogas, the American ethnographer, made the first recording of Siberian shamans (Chukchees) in 1901, his recording device picked up voices of unknown origin.[145]

Understanding such connections, Thomas Edison (1847–1931), the legendary American inventor, tried to build a machine to talk to the dead. Interestingly, Edison's parents were Spiritualists.[526, 48]

Several decades later, George Meek and William O'Neil claimed that they managed to construct such a device. Called a "Spiricom," they claimed that it allowed two-way communication with the dead.[305, 145, 936, 580]

Using technology to communicate with the dead is called instrumental transcommunication. If the procedure is real, contact with the dead is possible with radios, televisions, computers, video recorders, and telephones.

Modern instrumental transcommunication dates back to 1959, with the work of Friedrich Jurgenson.[305, 145] While recording bird noises, Jurgenson recorded the voice of his deceased mother relaying a message to him.[305, 145, 48] At first, he thought the voices were extraterrestrials. He published *Voices from the Universe* in 1964 and *Radio Contact with the Dead* in 1967.[48]

Interestingly, one kind of crystal, silicon, is at the heart of our electronics industry,[915] and occultism has long considered crystals to be magical. Believed to be connected to the "sky world and the rainbow," traditional cultures view crystals as "holy ice" or "solidified light."[266, 265]

Radio

One technique, this one used by Marcello Bacci, uses a shortwave radio (preferably one with old-fashioned vacuum tubes). Turn the dial until you hear white noise resembling the sound of the wind. The white noise should not be too loud or too soft. Turn on a recorder. Voices unheard by the ear may be collected by the recorder.[305, 145]

With the Bacci technique, one to four radios may be used. If multiple radios are used, set each to a different "white noise."[145] Dr. Anabela Cardoso, a Portuguese scholar who has extensively used the technique, prefers to use a shortwave radio set to 14 MHz and an AM radio set to 1500 kHz.[145]

Place the devices in a quiet room. Use the recorder to record the whole session. The microphone should be positioned between one and two yards from the white noise.[145]

Conduct three sessions each week, always at the same time of day or night. Each session should last no more than ten to fifteen minutes.[145]

Between each question, wait one or two minutes. Do not ask about the future. In the beginning, ask questions with simple answers, such as "yes" or "no." Later, with experience, more complex questions may be asked.[145]

According to Dr. Cardoso, communication is possible only with dead people who had a previous interaction or relationship with us while they were alive.[145]

Curiously, the largest number of communications will come through at the time of the waxing moon. There will be fewer communications at the full moon, even fewer at the dark moon, and the fewest at the waning moon.[145]

Video

A second technique, called the "psychoimages method," was developed in 1985 by Klaus Schreiber and Martin Wenzel. This method involves a video camera and a television in a "closed loop."[145]

Tune a television to a blank channel. Connect the video camera to the television, and record the "snow" on the screen. This will project the result back onto the screen so that it can be filmed again in a continual feedback loop.[145]

When the video is later viewed frame by frame, images sometimes may be seen. (Researchers have seen landscapes, people, and allegedly "higher beings."[145])

Because the video must be viewed frame by frame, use this method only for a few minutes each session.[145]

Telephone Calls from the Dead

The telephone system is a machine that literally covers the entire planet. Everything is now penetrated by the telephone network.[915]

Telephone calls from the dead usually are unsolicited and they occur unexpectedly. The ring is often odd, and may be abnormally elongated.

The call will not show up in the telephone records, indicating that the user's telephone is haunted, not the whole network.[733, 737]

The telephone calls usually occur within a day of the death of the caller, but there are reports of calls coming through years later.[737, 526]

If the called person is aware of the caller's death, the called person may be too shocked to speak or may even hang up.[526, 737] If there is a conversation, often the call ends when the line abruptly goes dead.[737]

Haunted Computers

Like haunted telephones, haunted computer contact is usually unexpected. The contact is not solicited.

The most famous case occurred in 1984. Kenneth Webster, living in Wales, received (via several different computers) 250 communications from a person who allegedly lived in the sixteenth century. The messages were in a Tudor-era dialect, and personal details provided by the alleged spirit were later confirmed by library research.[916] Interestingly, the contact occurred before the Internet, so there was no contact with other computers.[124]

The Webster case is described in a book, *The Vertical Plane*,[916] and it is also the subject of a British television documentary.

Afterword

At my age, I can see into the future much better than I can recall the past.

CHINESE SAGE

Let it be as it is and as it was from the beginning.

PAUSANIAS

To me belongs yesterday; I know tomorrow.

BOOK OF THE DEAD (EGYPTIAN)

I've died before and it was really quite pleasant. . . . It's the getting there that hurts.

DANNION BRINKLEY,
SAVED BY THE LIGHT

There are reports of rare individuals who never taste death. China, for example, has the legend of the Eight Immortals.[207] Unlike the gods, who inhabit extraterrestrial regions, the Eight Immortals usually live on three hidden islands named P'ang Tai, Fang Tchang, and Ying Tcheou. On occasion, however, the Immortals are seen in one of our cities, where they move about disguised as ordinary humans.[207]

The Japanese have the Sokushinbutsu. Believed to be in suspended animation, these individuals starve themselves in a special rite of "self-mummification." Seated in a lotus posture, they will awaken when the Buddha Maitreya, the future Buddha, comes to earth.[86] The last "self-mummified" person has been waiting since 1868.[86]

The Mormons have the tradition of the "Three Nephites." Described in the *Book of Mormon,* these men were given immortality by Jesus, and allegedly they wander the earth and assist people.[301]

The Mormons also believe that the Apostle John still walks the earth today and performs acts of goodness. In chapter 21 of the Gospel of John, Jesus promises that John will live until the Christ returns.[800, 301, 934]

More remarkably, the Hindus speak of Markandeya—the young boy who never dies. He lived in the last universe, and now he lives in this universe. On occasion, pious Hindus see him.[442]

Most likely, however, virtually all of us will die, putrefy, and turn to dust.

Indeed, at the time I write these words, 150,000 humans on earth die *every day.* In the time you take to read this sentence, at least ten people will die.[424]

For some, death can be peaceful. The Buddha—the "awakened one"—the teacher of man and the teacher of the gods[963]—lay on his right side, and in complete lucidity and composure, died.[637]

For others, death can be gruesome. When Oscar Wilde (1854–1900) expired, his body exploded with blood and pus from every orifice. Syphilis may have been the cause.[668]

For most humans, however, there is the ugliness of the ordinary death. The novelist Joseph Conrad (1857–1924) wrote these haunting words:

> I have wrestled with death. It is the most unexciting contest you
> can imagine. It takes place in an impalpable greyness, with noth-
> ing underfoot, with nothing around, without spectators, without

clamor, without glory, without the great desire of victory, without the great fear of defeat, in a sickly atmosphere of tepid skepticism, without much belief in your own right, and still less in that of your adversary.[177]

Death does seem to be inescapable. In the words of Aleister Crowley (1875–1947), the occult writer, "Every man is a condemned criminal, only he does not know the date of his execution."[191]

In ancient lore, even the gods die. The grave of Zeus was on Crete, Cronus was buried in Sicily, Hermes was buried in Hermopolis, Aphrodite's grave was in Cyprus, Ares was buried in Greece, and Apollo, in one account, was buried at Delphi.[314]

And so, dear reader, you will die.

In effect, you are caught in a game that we are all forced to play, and in that game, according to Blaise Pascal (1623–1662), the great mathematician and one of the fathers of probability theory, you have only two options.[676] I *paraphrase* those options here:

Option ONE: you may wager that there is no afterlife, and live only for this world and no other. If you place your bet on this option, and you are correct, you win absolutely nothing, because everyone ends up the same.

Option TWO: you may wager that there is an afterlife, and prepare yourself for the otherworld by believing rightly and acting appropriately. If you are correct—and there is an afterlife—you will win a huge jackpot—a priceless treasure—perhaps an eternity in paradise.

Based on probability theory alone, the ONLY sensible wager is option two.

Chose rightly, my friend, and may we one day meet on the other side. Until then, in the words of the Celtic epic formula, "may the blessing of gods and non-gods be upon you."[794]

A Quick Guide to a Good Death

The Tibetan Way of Death

As a person dies, the Tibetans guide his thoughts. Just as past thinking has determined our present status, so our present thinking (at death) will determine our future status.

As a person dies, he must not sleep, faint, or fall into a coma. According to the Tibetans, a person who dies in that state will become confused, and when he awakens on the other side, he will not realize that he is dead.[208]

The dying person must not be given drugs or painkillers. The mind must remain clear. According to Lama Lodru, a Tibetan sage, "When a body is in a drugged condition, the mind, veiled with stupidity, cannot concentrate, and is easily drawn into the animal realm."[533]

Also, it is absolutely essential for the dying person to remain calm. Since the experiences in the next world (as in this world) are generated by our minds, dying with a disturbed mind or in a state of anger will cause problems, just as falling asleep "in an agitated state" leads to "nightmares."[363]

As a person dies, the Tibetans turn him over on to his right side. This is called the "Lying Posture of the Lion." Pressing the "throbbing of the arteries" on the right and left side of the neck will help the dying man's consciousness to exit from the "Brahmanic opening" on the top of the head. That leads to a higher rebirth.[663]

During the entire process of death, a monk will read from the *Bardo Thodol,* the celebrated Tibetan text.[207, 663]

Reincarnation

Some Possibilities

According to Professor Johannes Bronkhorst, "A belief in rebirth, *unlike the belief in karmic retribution,* is widespread in the world." (The italics are mine.)[120, 109, 71]

Interestingly, modern reincarnation research indicates that a person's next body may be determined by random factors, such as location at the time of death and the proximity of available bodies.[71, 109]

As Professor Carl B. Becker indicates in his classic *Paranormal Experience and Survival of Death,* there is some evidence in support of the following:[71]

1. Story's Law: People are usually reborn a few hundred miles from the sites of their deaths.
2. Evans-Wentz's Law: People will reincarnate in ways they believe are possible. For example, if they believe that a sex change is impossible in rebirth, they shall come back as the same gender.
3. Parker's Law: Violent death or unfulfilled cravings or desires for things of this life may be the primary causes of reincarnation.
4. Martinus's Law: People who die in childhood are reborn relatively quickly, but adults who die must spend a longer period in some intermediate state.

How to Have an Out-of-Body Experience

In an out-of-body experience, or OBE, the mind, the locus of our visual, auditory, and mental activities, leaves the body.[71] By merely willing, one can travel great distances and pass through objects.[71, 310, 606, 607, 595, 596]

The activity is *not* a type of hallucination. Hallucinations persist whether the eyes are open or closed, but out-of-body experiences will end when the eyes are opened.[71]

Interestingly, Professor Ken Ring studied blind people reporting out-of-body experiences, and the blind could see in the OBE state.[305]

A person having an OBE can visit any place in this world—in this universe—or in the afterworld. To go to a destination, one must only think it. To return to the body, one must only think that.[310, 606, 607, 595, 596]

According to tradition, Odin, the Norse god, had this power. In the *Ynglinga Saga,* Snorri Sturluson (1179–1241 CE) writes that Odin's body would lie "as if dead, or asleep," but he would "be off in a twinkling to distant lands upon his own or other people's business."[831]

In the modern era, famous practitioners of the OBE include Oliver Fox (1885-1949),[319] Sylvan Muldoon (1903–1969),[606, 607] and Robert Monroe (1915–1995).[594, 595, 596]

INFLUENTIAL FACTORS

Some out-of-body experiences occur in normal sleep.[70] Some occur in waking moments, while the body continues to walk or write.[70]

Most commonly, an OBE occurs at the moment of a serious accident, explosion, or shock.[70]

The OBE may be assisted by anesthesia, or narcotics such as peyote,[70] or drugs such as ketamine.[306]

Austerities, such as starvation, sexual deprivation (chastity), meditation, prolonged chanting, and whirling dances, may produce an OBE.[70] Sensory deprivation may also produce an OBE,[70] and so can lucid dreaming.[305]

There are many ways to willfully induce an OBE; what follows is one technique:[305]

> Naked, rest on a bed, with the right elbow touching the bed. Keep your right forearm raised in the air, so that if you fall asleep the forearm will fall and awaken you.
>
> Make yourself aware of the sensation of your body against the blankets.
>
> Imagine your body sinking through the bed. In time, after perhaps months of practice, you will find yourself out of your body.

Sylvan Muldoon used the following technique:[606, 607, 305]

> Imagine that you are looking at your own body from a position outside it.
>
> Or, imagine looking at a mirror image of yourself sitting opposite yourself.
>
> With practice, at some point your consciousness will transfer to the image.

APPENDIX IV

A Séance Procedure
to Contact the Dead

Tonight we attempt to contact the restless dead. We seek souls that are trapped in time, conscious of loss, and filled with hatred from life, that have not yet completely separated from our world.

According to the ancient Greeks, those who died an abnormal death, such as murder victims, executed criminals, and soldiers, are the restless dead.

Contact with the dead may occur in various ways.

Sometimes, direct contact during a séance is possible. The spirit may be perceived through any sense. A scent (the sense of smell is the most emotive of our senses) is the most common contact. The next most common manifestation is through the sense of touch (a cold spot may be perceived, most commonly on the left side). The third most common manifestation is through the sense of hearing (a sound or a voice). The rarest contact is visual, seeing a light or an apparition.[462]

Of course, a spirit may be present and be unknown to us. There are signs, however. When a candle flame burns blue, a spirit is present.[212, 780]

Also, the modern era has shown some connection between the dead and electronic equipment, so contact may occur during the séance through those items.[145]

Most commonly, if the séance procedure is successful, the ghost will appear to someone who sleeps in the house tonight. Iamblichus, the ancient scholar, said that the state between sleeping and waking is especially favorable to the reception of visions.[237]

In particular, the persons sleeping in the house should be prepared for what are called "hypnopompic" experiences. Described by F. W. H. Myers in 1901, hypnopompic experiences, unlike dreams, are startling and are apt to be remembered. When the eyes first open from sleep, an entity—totally solid—may be seen in the room. This may cause terror.[611, 755]

HELPFUL CONDITIONS

To contact a spirit, certain conditions are helpful. Although ghosts may be seen at any time (Tibetan séances do *not* require darkness),[208] specters are most visible at night. According to the Viking sagas, light weakens the dead.

The presence of moving water—such as a stream or a river—is helpful. According to tradition, ghosts cannot cross moving water, so they tend to gather adjacent to such places.[312, 122]

Strong emotions—especially anger and terror—draw spirits. A drop of fresh blood also draws spirits. (In contrast, menstrual blood, or the "red pollution,"[86] draws demons, and that is the reason pacts with the devil are traditionally signed with menstrual blood.)

If animals are in the room, they should be either female or castrated. The ancient Greeks thought that the dead had an affinity to such creatures.[330]

SETTING UP A SÉANCE

Four people—or six or more—must sit around a wooden table. There cannot be five people, for Christ was murdered with five wounds, and five (symbolized by the pentagon and the pentacle) draws sinister forces. (The victims of Jack the Ripper—in nineteenth-century London—were positioned to form a huge pentagon in the city.)

One person must be designated as the medium, the person leading the séance. Anyone may be used as a medium, but Iamblichus recommended a young and simple person.[439] Others believe that the best medium is a mature female past childbearing years. For paranormal contact, the Vikings preferred post-menstrual women whose only meat was animal hearts.[380]

The hands of the people in the séance must be placed flat on the table, with the hands of each person touching the hands of the people on either side of them. Throughout the procedure, do not break the circle by moving your hands.

In the center of the table, directly across from the medium, place a scrying device (an object with a reflective surface).

The Aztecs used a "smoky mirror" made from obsidian. One such Aztec scrying device, used by the great John Dee, is reputedly in the British Museum. Michel de Nostredame, the seer who was also called Nostradamus, used a bowl of blood or a bowl of water as a scrying device. In recent centuries, many people have used crystal balls.

As our scrying device, we use a mirror, tilted at an angle so that the medium cannot *see her own face*. Throughout the procedure, the medium will focus her attention on the mirror.[598]

Two burning candles made from tallow (animal fat) must be positioned on the north and south sides of the mirror. (Do not be concerned about the use of animal fat. In Buddhism, the sin belongs only to the killer.)[589]

Each candle must be marked with a small sample of fresh blood. According to Porphyry, fresh blood endows the dead with a semblance of life.

On the west side of the mirror, place a fragment of a natural magnet, also called a lodestone or bloodstone. Because magnets can move inanimate metallic objects, the Egyptians believed that magnets possess the life force.[114] This life force will help animate the dead.

On the east side of the mirror, place a book open to a necromantic procedure. One is found in the Bible (1 Samuel 28). Another is found in Virgil's *Aeneid*. Still another is found in the "Voluspa," in the *Eddaic Verses*.

Outside the séance circle—on the west side of the room—place an audio recorder and a radio set to "white noise." If possible, use an old-fashioned vacuum-tube radio. Afterward, listen to the recording for evidence of spectral voices.[145]

Also, outside the circle, place a television and a video recorder. Turn the television on and tune it to a blank channel. Connect the video camera to the television and position the camera so that it records the "snow" on the screen, thereby creating a closed loop. After the séance, when the video is viewed in slow motion, one frame at a time, faces may be seen.[145]

Protection

In case of misadventure, protections are available.

If the apparition seems threatening, speak Latin. Francis Grose, an eighteenth-century expert, said that Latin terrifies even an "audacious ghost."[122]

For additional protection, position graveyard earth outside the circle. If anyone feels threatened by a specter, throw grave earth into its face. According to legend, a ghost touched by grave earth will become docile and must obey commands.[122]

Finally, position a dagger outside the circle. According to Sir James Frazer, iron is obnoxious to otherworldly beings.[314]

Séance Protocol

Before starting, ring a necromancy bell. This is a bell that has rested seven days and seven nights on a grave. Such a bell has the power to awaken the dead.[38]

During the séance, do not speak. Only the designated medium may speak.

While leading the séance, the medium must keep her mind clear. She must not try to think, but should let all thoughts freely enter her mind.[305]

No drugs should be used by the medium. According to Professor Mircea Eliade, drugs are used only in the decadent stages of shamanism.[266]

Everyone must remain serious and respectful. Above all, do not laugh. According to legend, the dead cannot laugh with joy and therefore levity offends them.[111]

During the séance, each participant must focus on the medium or the items at the center of the table.

According to Professor David Fontana, in spectacular séances, a transfiguration will occur, and a transparent spirit face will form over the medium's face.[305]

During the séance, remember that contact may be perceived through any sense. Be aware of scents, feelings, sounds, and sights.

When the medium is finished, she must thank the spirits. She must then close the book and extinguish the candles.

Before people depart into the night, they must be purified with brimstone (sulphur).

FINIS

Bibliography

Editor's note: The author has drawn on 965 sources in the creation of this book, texts from around the globe and throughout time. A large portion of these source texts have been published multiple times, by different publishers and in different periods of time. Because of this, only author names and book titles are listed in this bibliography rather than a specific edition or printing.

1. Abanes, Richard. *Becoming Gods: A Closer Look at 21st-Century Mormonism.*
2. Abbot, Elizabeth. *A History of Celibacy.*
3. Abbott, Edwin A. *Flatland: A Romance of Many Dimensions.*
4. Abel, Ernest L. *Death Gods: An Encyclopedia of the Rulers, Evil Spirits, and Geographies of the Dead.*
5. Abhedananda, Cornelius. *On Reincarnation: Vedanta Philosophy.*
6. Abraham, Philip. *Curiosities of Judaism: Facts, Opinions, Anecdotes and Remarks Relative to the Hebrew Nation.*
7. Acikyildiz, Birgül. *The Yezidis: The History of a Community, Culture and Religion.*
8. *Acts of Thomas.*
9. Addison, James Thayer. *Life Beyond Death in the Beliefs of Mankind.*
10. Aeschylus. *Eumenides.*
11. Agrippa von Nettesheim, Henry Cornelius. *Fourth Book of Occult Philosophy.*
12. Agrippa von Nettesheim, Henry Cornelius. *Three Books of Occult Philosophy.*
13. Aguilar-Moreno, Manuel. *Handbook to Life in the Aztec World.*
14. *Aitareya Brahmana.*
15. Akerley, Ben Edward. *The X-Rated Bible: An Irreverent Survey of Sex in the Scriptures.*

16. Al Da'mi, Muhammad. *The Other Spiritualities of the Middle East: The Minority Religious Traditions of the Ahl-E Haqq, the Mandaeans and the Yezidis.*

17. Alexander, Jane. *The Body, Mind, Spirit Miscellany: The Ultimate Collection of Fascinations, Facts, Truths, and Insights.*

18. Alexander, Joseph H. *Utmost Savagery: The Three Days of Tarawa.*

19. Al-Shawi, Ibrahim. *A Glimpse of Iraq.*

20. Andrews, Carol. *Egyptian Mummies.*

21. Andrews, Edward Denning. *The People Called Shakers.*

22. Angus, S. *The Mystery-Religions.*

23. Anonymous. *Jainism: Short Essays on Jain Philosophy.*

24. Anonymous. *Phantoms of the Deep, or Legends and Superstitions of the Sea and of Sailors.*

25. Anonymous. *Pistis: Reology, the Three Grand Illusions, and the Power to Choose.*

26. Anthony, David W. *The Horse, the Wheel, and Language: How Bronze-Age Riders from the Eurasian Steppes Shaped the Modern World.*

27. Apollodorus. *The Library of Greek Mythology.*

28. Ariès, Philippe. *Western Attitudes toward Death: From the Middle Ages to the Present.*

29. Aristotle. *On the Soul.*

30. Armstrong, Karen. *A History of God: The 4,000-Year Quest of Judaism, Christianity and Islam.*

31. Armstrong, Karen. *Islam: A Short History.*

32. Armstrong, Karen. *A Short History of Myth.*

33. Ashley, Leonard R. N. *The Complete Book of Devils and Demons.*

34. Ashley, Leonard R. N. *The Complete Book of Dreams: And What They Mean.*

35. Ashley, Leonard R. N. *The Complete Book of Ghosts and Poltergeists.*

36. Ashley, Leonard R. N. *The Complete Book of Magic and Witchcraft.*

37. Ashley, Leonard R. N. *The Complete Book of Sex Magic.*

38. Ashley, Leonard R. N. *The Complete Book of Spells, Curses and Magical Recipes.*

39. Ashley, Leonard R. N. *The Complete Book of the Devil's Disciples.*

40. Ashley, Leonard R. N. *The Complete Book of Vampires.*

41. Assmann, Jan. *Death and Salvation in Ancient Egypt.*

42. Assmann, Jan. *The Search for God in Ancient Egypt.*

43. Atack, Jon. *A Piece of Blue Sky: Scientology, Dianetics and L. Ron Hubbard Exposed.*

44. Atwater, P. M. H. *The Big Book of Near Death Experiences: The Ultimate Guide to What Happens When We Die.*

45. Auboyer, Jeannine. *Daily Life in Ancient India: From Approximately 200 BC to 700 AD.*
46. Avalon, Arthur. *The Serpent Power: The Secrets of Tantric and Shaktic Yoga.*
47. *Avesta: The Religious Books of the Parsees.* 3 vols.
48. Aykroyd, Peter H. *History of Ghosts: The True Story of Séances, Mediums, Ghosts, and Ghostbusters.*
49. Badger, George Percy. *An Inquiry into the Religious Tenets of the Yezeedees.*
50. Baldick, Julian. *Animal and Shaman: Ancient Religions of Central Asia.*
51. Barber, Malcolm. *The Cathars: Dualist Heretics in Languedoc in the High Middle Ages.*
52. Barber, Paul. *Vampires, Burial, and Death: Folklore and Reality.*
53. Barber, Richard. *The Holy Grail: Imagination and Belief.*
54. Barbour, Julian. *The End of Time: The Next Revolution in Physics.*
55. Barfield, Thomas. *The Nomadic Alternative.*
56. Baring-Gould, Sabine. *Strange Survivals.*
57. Barnstone, Willis. *The Other Bible.*
58. Barrett, David V. *A Brief Guide to Secret Religions.*
59. Barrett, David V. *A Brief History of Secret Societies: An Unbiased History of our Desire for Secret Knowledge.*
60. Barrett, David V. *The New Believers: Sects, 'Cults' and Alternative Religions.*
61. Barrett, Francis. *The Magus: A Complete System of Occult Philosophy.*
62. Basham, A. L. *History and Doctrines of the Ajivikas.*
63. Basham, A. L. *The Origins and Development of Classical Hinduism.*
64. Basham, A. L. *The Wonder That Was India.*
65. Baskin, Wade. *Dictionary of Satanism.*
66. Baudelaire, Charles. *Baudelaire, His Prose and Poetry.*
67. Baudrillard, Jean. *Fragments: Cool Memories III, 1990–1995.*
68. Bayless, Raymond. *Apparitions and Survival of Death.*
69. Beard, Mary, John North, and Simon Price. *Religions of Rome.* Vol. 1.
70. Becker, Carl B. *Breaking the Circle: Death and the Afterlife in Buddhism.*
71. Becker, Carl B. *Paranormal Experience and Survival of Death.*
72. Bendann, Effie. *Death Customs: An Analytical Study of Burial Rites.*
73. Bender, A. P. "Beliefs, Rites, Burial, and Customs of the Jews, Connected with Death, Burial, and Mourning." *The Jewish Quarterly Review.*
74. Benson, Richard, and Cindy Benson. *Secrets Mormons Don't Want You to Know.*
75. Bernabe, Alberto, and Ana Isabel San Cristobal. *Instructions for the Netherworld: The Orphic Gold Tablets.*
76. Bernal, J. D. *Science in History.* 4 vols.
77. Besterman, Theodore. *Crystal-Gazing.*

78. Betts, Robert Benton. *The Druze.*
79. Bevan, Edwyn. *Sibyls and Seers: A Survey of Some Ancient Theories of Revelation and Inspiration.*
80. Bhagavad Gita.
81. *Bhagavata Purana.*
82. *Bhavishya Purana.*
83. Bible.
84. Binet-Sanglé, Charles. *La Folie de Jésus.*
85. Black, Jonathan. *The Secret History of Dante: Unearthing the Mysteries of the Inferno.*
86. Blacker, Carmen. *The Catalpa Bow: A Study of Shamanistic Practices in Japan.*
87. Blackman, Sushila, ed. *Graceful Exits: How Great Beings Die: Death Stories of Tibetan, Hindu and Zen Masters.*
88. Blake, William. *The Marriage of Heaven and Hell.*
89. Blatty, William Peter. *The Exorcist.*
90. Blavatsky, Helena Petrovna. *Isis Unveiled.* 2 vols.
91. Blavatsky, Helena Petrovna. *The Secret Doctrine: The Synthesis of Science, Religion, and Philosophy.* 2 vols.
92. Blofeld, John. *Taoism: The Road to Immortality.*
93. Blom, Jan Dirk. *A Dictionary of Hallucinations.*
94. Bloom, Mia. *Dying to Kill: The Allure of Suicide Terror.*
95. Boase, T. S. R. *Death in the Middle Ages: Mortality, Judgment, and Remembrance.*
96. Bodhidharma. *The Zen Teaching of Bodhidharma.*
97. Bondeon, Jan. *Buried Alive: The Terrifying History of Our Most Primal Fear.*
98. Bonfante, Larissa. *Etruscan Life and Afterlife: A Handbook of Etruscan Studies.*
99. *Book of Arda Viraf.*
100. *Book of Mormon.*
101. *Book of Thomas the Contender.*
102. Borges, Jorge Luis. *Collected Fictions.*
103. Bova, Ben. *Immortality: How Science Is Extending Your Life Span—And Changing the World.*
104. Bowden, Hugh. *Mystery Cults of the Ancient World.*
105. Bowker, John. *The Meanings of Death.*
106. Boyce, Mary. *Zoroastrians: Their Religious Beliefs and Practices.*
107. Bragg, Lois. *Oedipus Borealis: The Aberrant Body in Old Icelandic Myth and Saga.*
108. *Brahmavaivarta Purana.*

109. Bramley, William. *The Gods of Eden.*
110. Brazier, Chris. *The No-Nonsense Guide to World History.*
111. Bremmer, Jan. *The Early Greek Concept of the Soul.*
112. Bremmer, Jan. *The Rise and Fall of the Afterlife.*
113. Brennan, J. H. *Tibetan Magic and Mysticism.*
114. Brier, Bob. *Ancient Egyptian Magic.*
115. Brier, Bob. *Egyptomania: Our Three Thousand Year Obsession with the Land of the Pharaohs.*
116. Brier, Bob, and Hoyt Hobbs. *Daily Life of the Ancient Egyptians.*
117. *Brihadaranyaka Upanishad.*
118. Bringsvaerd, Tor. *Phantoms and Fairies from Norwegian Folklore.*
119. Brinkley, Dannion, with Paul Perry. *Saved by the Light: The True Story of a Man Who Died Twice and the Profound Revelations He Received.*
120. Bronkhorst, Johannes. *Karma.*
121. Brown, Jonathan A. C. *Muhammad: A Very Short Introduction.*
122. Brown, Theo. *Fate of the Dead: Study in Folk Eschatology in the West Country after the Reformation.*
123. Browne, Thomas. *Religio Medici and Urne-Buriall.*
124. Buckland, Raymond. *The Spirit Book: The Encyclopedia of Clairvoyance, Channeling, and Spirit Communication.*
125. Budge, E. A. Wallis. *Babylonian Life and History.*
126. Budge, E. A. Wallis. *The Egyptian Book of the Dead: The Papyrus of Ani in the British Museum.*
127. Budge, E. A. Wallis. *Egyptian Ideas of the Afterlife.*
128. Budge, E. A. Wallis. *Egyptian Magic.*
129. Burkert, Walter. *Ancient Mystery Cults.*
130. Burkert, Walter. *Greek Religion: Archaic and Classical.*
131. Burkert, Walter. *Homo Necans: The Anthropology of Ancient Greek Sacrificial Ritual and Myth.*
132. Burnfield, David. *Patristic Universalism: An Alternative to the Traditional View of Divine Judgment.*
133. Burton, Rulon T. *We Believe: Doctrines and Principles of the Church of Jesus Christ of Latter Day Saints.*
134. Buruma, Ian, and Avishai Margalit, *Occidentalism: The West in the Eyes of Its Enemies.*
135. Butler, Elizabeth M. *Ritual Magic.*
136. Bynum, Caroline Walker. *Resurrection of the Body in Western Christianity, 200–1336.*
137. Calmet, Augustin. *The Phantom World; Or, The Philosophy of Spirits, Apparitions.*

138. Campbell, Joseph. *The Hero with a Thousand Faces.*
139. Campbell, Joseph. *The Masks of God.* 4 vols.
140. Campbell, Joseph. *Transformations of Myth through Time.*
141. Campbell, Robert Allen. *Phallic Worship: An Outline of the Worship of the Generative Organs.*
142. Campion, Nardi Reeder. *Mother Ann Lee: Morning Star of the Shakers.*
143. Camporesi, Piero. *Fear of Hell: Images of Damnation and Salvation in Early Modern Europe.*
144. Camporesi, Piero. *Juice of Life: The Symbolic and Magic Significance of Blood.*
145. Cardoso, Anabela. *Electronic Voices: Contact with Another Dimension?*
146. Carlson, Ron. *Fast Facts on False Teachings.*
147. Carmody, Denise Lardner. *The Oldest God: Archaic Religion Yesterday and Today.*
148. Carpini, Giovanni. *The Story of the Mongols Whom We Call the Tartars.*
149. Carrasco, David. *Daily Life of the Aztecs: People of the Sun and Earth.*
150. Carrasco, David. *Religions of Mesoamerica: Cosmovision and Ceremonial Centers.*
151. Carroll, Sean. *From Eternity to Here: The Quest for the Ultimate Theory of Time.*
152. Carter, Jesse Benedict. *Religion of Numa.*
153. Carter, John. *Sex and Rockets: The Occult World of Jack Parsons.*
154. Cartledge, Paul. *The Spartans: The World of the Warrior-Heroes of Ancient Greece.*
155. Carus, Paul. *History of the Devil and the Idea of Evil.*
156. Caso, Alfonso. *The Aztecs: People of the Sun.*
157. Catlin, George. *North American Indians.*
158. Chadwick, H. M. *The Cult of Othin: An Essay in the Ancient Religion of the North.*
159. Chakravarti, Mahadev. *Concept of Rudra-Siva Through the Ages.*
160. Chamberlin, Russell. *The Bad Popes.*
161. Chambers, Robert W. *The King in Yellow and Other Horror Stories.*
162. *Chandogya Upanishad.*
163. Chuang Tzu. *Basic Writings.*
164. Chuvin, Pierre. *A Chronicle of the Last Pagans.*
165. Cicero. *The Nature of the Gods.*
166. Cicero. *On Divination.*
167. Clauss, Manfred. *The Roman Cult of Mithras: The God and His Mysteries.*
168. Clegg, Brian. *How to Build a Time Machine: The Real Science of Time Travel.*

169. Clendinnen, Inga. *Aztecs: An Interpretation*.
170. Cobo, Bernabe. *Inca Religion and Customs*.
171. *Codex Vaticanus A*
172. *Codex Vaticanus B*.
173. Codrington, Robert Henry. *The Melanesians: Studies in Their Anthropology and Folklore*.
174. Cohen, Martin Samuel, ed. *The Shi'ur Qomah: Texts and Recensions*.
175. Coleman, Charles. *The Mythology of the Hindus*.
176. Comte, Fernand. *Mythology*.
177. Conrad, Joseph. *Heart of Darkness*.
178. Coombes, Anne. *Belarus*.
179. Coon, Carlton S. *The Hunting Peoples*.
180. Cooper, D. Jason. *Mithras: Mysteries and Initiation Rediscovered*.
181. Corliss, William R. *Biological Anomalies: Humans II*.
182. Cornaro, Luigi. *The Art of Living Long*.
183. Cornelius, J. Edward. *Aleister Crowley and the Ouija Board*.
184. Cort, John E. *Jains in the World: Religious Values and Ideology in India*.
185. Couprie, Dirk L. *Heaven and Earth in Ancient Greek Cosmology: From Thales to Heraclides Ponticus*.
186. Cowan, James. *Mysteries of the Dream-Time: The Spiritual Life of Australian Aborigines*.
187. Craigie, W. A. *The Religion of Ancient Scandinavia*.
188. Crookall, Robert. *Intimations of Immortality*.
189. Crookes, William. *Researches in the Phenomena of Spiritualism*.
190. Crowell, Eugene. *Spirit World: Its Inhabitants, Nature, and Philosophy*.
191. Crowley, Aleister. *Book 4*.
192. Crowley, Aleister. *Book of the Law*.
193. Crowley, Aleister. *The Book of Lies*.
194. Crowley, Aleister. *Magick without Tears*.
195. Crowley, Aleister, and Scott Michaelsen, ed. *Portable Darkness: An Aleister Crowley Reader*.
196. Curran, Bob. *Lost Lands, Forgotten Realms*.
197. Cytowic, Richard E. *The Man Who Tasted Shapes*.
198. Czaplicka, M. A. *Shamanism in Siberia*.
199. Dainton, Barry. *Time and Space*.
200. Dalal, Roshen. *The Religions of India: A Concise Guide to Nine Major Faiths*.
201. Dandelion, Ben Pink. *An Introduction to Quakerism*.
202. Daniélou, Alain. *The Myths and Gods of India: The Classic Work on Hindu Polytheism*.

203. Daniélou, Alain. *The Phallus: Sacred Symbol of Male Creative Power.*

204. Daniélou, Alain. *While the Gods Play: Shaiva Oracles and Predictions on the Cycles of History and the Destiny of Mankind.*

205. Darwin, Charles. *The Descent of Man.*

206. Davenport, Guy. *Herakleitos and Diogenes.*

207. David-Neel, Alexandra. *Immortality and Reincarnation: Wisdom from the Forbidden Journey.*

208. David-Neel, Alexandra. *Magic and Mystery in Tibet.*

209. Davies, Jon. *Death, Burial, and Rebirth in the Religions of Antiquity.*

210. Davies, Nigel. *Human Sacrifice in History and Today.*

211. Davies, Owen. *Grimoires: A History of Magic Books.*

212. Davies, Owen. *The Haunted: A Social History of Ghosts.*

213. Davies, Owen. *Magic: A Very Short Introduction.*

214. Davies, Owen. *Paganism: A Very Short Introduction.*

215. Davies, Paul. *How to Build a Time Machine.*

216. Davis, Andrew Jackson. *The Harmonial Philosophy.*

217. Dayan, Joan. *Haiti, History, and the Gods.*

218. De Coulanges, Fustel. *The Ancient City: A Study on the Religion, Laws and Institutions of Greece and Rome.*

219. De Grummond, Nancy Thomson. *Etruscan Myth, Sacred History, and Legend.*

220. De Grummond, Nancy Thomson, and Erika Simon, eds. *The Religion of the Etruscans.*

221. De Landa, Diego. *Yucatan Before and After the Conquest.*

222. De Mello, Margo. *Faces around the World.*

223. De Plancy, Collin. *Dictionnaire Infernal.*

224. De Sade, Marquis. *Justine, or the Misfortunes of Virtue.*

225. De Sade, Marquis. *Philosophy in the Boudoir.*

226. De Sahagun, Bernardino. *General History of the Things of New Spain (Florentine Codex).*

227. De Santillana, Giorgio, and Hertha von Dechend. *Hamlet's Mill: An Essay Investigating the Origins of Human Knowledge and Its Transmission through Myth.*

228. Defoe, Daniel. *An Essay on the History and Reality of Apparitions.*

229. Deren, Maya. *Divine Horsemen: The Living Gods of Haiti.*

230. Descartes. *Meditations.*

231. Devereux, Paul. *The Long Trip: A Prehistory of Psychedelia.*

232. Dhalla, Maneckji Nusservanji. *Zoroastrian Theology from the Earliest Times to the Present Day.*

233. *Dhammapada.*

234. *Dialogue between Hermes Trismegistus and Asclepius.*

235. Dimashqi, Al-Hafiz Ibn Kathir. *Book of the End—Great Trials and Tribulations.*

236. Dio, Lucius Cassius. *Roman History.*

237. Dodds, E. R. *The Greeks and the Irrational.*

238. Doniger, Wendy. *The Hindus: An Alternative History.*

239. Dorgan, Howard. *In the Hands of a Happy God: The "No-Hellers" of Central Appalachia.*

240. Dowding, Hugh. *Many Mansions.*

241. Doyle, Arthur Conan. *The History of Spiritualism.*

242. Driver, Harold Edson. *Indians of North America.*

243. Drury, Nevill. *Stealing Fire from Heaven: The Rise of Modern Western Magic.*

244. Du Chaillu, Paul Belloni. *The Viking Age: The Early History, Manners, and Customs of the Ancestors of the English-Speaking Nations: Illustrated from the Antiquities Discovered.* 2 vols.

245. Dubois, J. A. *Hindu Manners, Customs and Ceremonies.*

246. Duffy, Eamon. *Saints and Sinners: A History of the Popes.*

247. Duffy, Kevin. *Who Were the Celts?*

248. Dumezil, Georges. *Gods of the Ancient Northmen.*

249. Dundas, Paul. *The Jains.*

250. Dunne, John S. *The City of the Gods: A Study in Myth and Mortality.*

251. Dunne, John W. *An Experiment with Time.*

252. Duthel, Heinz. *Nothing or Existence Is Not a Property.*

253. Eastman, Charles A. *The Soul of the Indian.*

254. Eddy, Mary Baker. *Science and Health with Key to the Scriptures.*

255. Edgerton, Robert. *Africa's Armies: From Honor to Infamy.*

256. Editors of Popular Science. *FYI (Popular Science): 229 Curious Questions Answered by the World's Smartest People.*

257. Edwards, Jonathan. *Sinners in the Hands of an Angry God.*

258. *Egyptian Coffin Texts.*

259. *Egyptian Pyramid Texts.*

260. Eisler, Robert. *Man into Wolf—An Anthropological Interpretation of Sadism, Masochism, and Lycanthropy.*

261. Eliade, Mircea. *A History of Religious Ideas.* 3 vols.

262. Eliade, Mircea. *Images and Symbols.*

263. Eliade, Mircea. *The Myth of the Eternal Return: Cosmos and History.*

264. Eliade, Mircea. *Occultism, Witchcraft, and Cultural Fashions: Essays in Comparative Religions.*

265. Eliade, Mircea. *Rites and Symbols of Initiation: The Mysteries of Birth and Rebirth.*

266. Eliade, Mircea. *Shamanism: Archaic Techniques of Ecstasy.*

267. Eliade, Mircea. *Yoga: Immortality and Freedom.*

268. Eliot, Alexander. *The Universal Myths.*

269. Ellis, A. B. *Yoruba-Speaking Peoples of the Slave Coast of West Africa.*

270. Ellis-Davidson, Hilda Roderick. *The Lost Beliefs of Northern Europe.*

271. Ellis-Davidson, Hilda Roderick. *Myths and Symbols in Pagan Europe: Early Scandinavian and Celtic Religions*

272. Ellis-Davidson, Hilda Roderick. *The Road to Hel: A Study of the Conception of the Dead in Old Norse Literature.*

273. Ellwood, Robert. *Tales of Lights and Shadows: Mythology of the Afterlife.*

274. Empson, R. H. W. *The Cult of the Peacock Angel: A Short Account of the Yezidi Tribes of Kurdistan.*

275. Engelstein, Laura. *Castration and the Heavenly Kingdom: A Russian Folktale.*

276. Ephiphanius of Salamis. *The Panarion.*

277. *Epic of Gilgamesh.*

278. Epicurus. *Letter to Menoeceus.*

279. Eraly, Abraham. *Gem in the Lotus: The Seeding of Indian Civilisation.*

280. Erman, Adolf. *Life in Ancient Egypt.*

281. Erricker, Clive. *Buddhism: An Introduction.*

282. Estep, Sarah Wilson. *Roads to Eternity.*

283. Ettinger, Robert C. W. *The Prospect of Immortality.*

284. Eusebius. *The Church History.*

285. Evans, Hilary. *Gods, Spirits, Cosmic Guardians: A Comparative Study of the Encounter Experience.*

286. Evans-Wentz, W. Y. *The Fairy-Faith in Celtic Countries.*

287. Evola, Julius. *Revolt Against the Modern World.*

288. *Eyrbyggja Saga.*

289. Fa-Hien. *Record of Buddhistic Kingdoms.*

290. Farr, Florence. *Egyptian Magic.*

291. Faustino, Mara. *Heaven and Hell: A Compulsively Readable Compendium of Myth, Legend, Wisdom, and Wit for Saints and Sinners.*

292. Fehlinger, Hans. *Sexual Life of Primitive People.*

293. Fehrenbach, T. R. *Comanches: The History of a People.*

294. Festugière, André Jean. *Epicurus and His Gods.*

295. Feuerstein, Georg, Subhash Kak, and David Frawley. *In Search of the Cradle of Civilization.*

296. Feuerstein, Georg. *Tantra: Path of Ecstasy.*

297. Feuerstein, Georg, and Roger Walsh. *Holy Madness: The Shock Tactics and Radical Teachings of Crazy-Wise Adepts, Holy Fools and Rascal Gurus.*

298. Figueira, Dorothy Matilda. *Aryans, Jews, Brahmins: Theorizing Authority through Myths of Identity.*
299. Finley, M. I. *The World of Odysseus.*
300. Finucane, R. C. *Ghosts.*
301. Fitzgerald, David. *The Complete Heretic's Guide to Western Religion Book One: The Mormons.*
302. Flammarion, Camille. *Lumen.*
303. Flower, Michael. *The Seer in Ancient Greece.*
304. Flowers, Stephen E. *Lords of the Left-Hand Path: Forbidden Practices and Spiritual Heresies.*
305. Fontana, David. *Is There An Afterlife?*
306. Fontana, David. *Life Beyond Death: What Should We Expect?*
307. Foote, G. W., and W. P. Ball. *The Bible Handbook.*
308. Fors, Andrew Peter. *The Ethical World-Conception of the Norse People.*
309. Fort, Charles. *Book of the Damned.*
310. Fox, Oliver. *Astral Projection.*
311. Fox, William Sherwood. *The Mythology of All Races. Greek and Roman.*
312. Frazer, James George. *The Belief in Immortality and the Worship of the Dead.* 3 vols.
313. Frazer, James George. *The Fear of the Dead in Primitive Religion.*
314. Frazer, James George. *The Golden Bough: A Study in Magic and Religion.*
315. Frazer, James George. "Putting Children on the Fire." (Appendix to his edition of Apollodorus, *Library*.)
316. Freixedo, Salvador. *Visionaries, Mystics, and Contactees.*
317. Freud, Sigmund. "Thought for the Times on War and Death."
318. Friedman, David M. *A Mind of Its Own: A Cultural History of the Penis.*
319. Fries, Jan. *Cauldron of the Gods: A Manual of Celtic Magick.*
320. Frobenius, Leo, and Eike Haberland, ed. *Frobenius on African History, Art and Culture.*
321. Fuller, John G. *The Great Soul Trial: The Gripping Story of the Prospector Who Left a Fortune to a Study of the Soul.*
322. Gardiner, Eileen. *Ancient Near Eastern Hell: Visions, Tours and Descriptions of the Infernal Otherworld.*
323. Gardiner, Eileen. *Egyptian Hell: Visions, Tours and Descriptions of the Infernal Otherworld.*
324. Gardiner, Eileen. *Hindu Hell: Visions, Tours and Descriptions of the Infernal Otherworld.*
325. Gardiner, Eileen. *Visions of Heaven and Hell Before Dante.*
326. Gardiner, Eileen. *Zoroastrian Hell: Visions, Tours and Descriptions of the Infernal Otherworld.*

327. Gardner, Gerald B. *The Meaning of Witchcraft*.

328. Gardner, Gerald. *Witchcraft Today*.

329. Garland, Robert. *Ancient Greece: Everyday Life in the Birthplace of Western Civilization*.

330. Garland, Robert. *The Greek Way of Death*.

331. Garland, Robert. *Religion and the Greeks*.

332. *Garuda Purana*.

333. Gibbon, Edward. *The Decline and Fall of the Roman Empire*.

334. Gibbon, Edward. *On Christianity*.

335. Gill, William Wyatt. *Myths and Songs from the South Pacific*.

336. Gilmore, George William. *Animism or Thought Currents of Primitive Peoples*.

337. Gimbutas, Marija. *The Gods and Goddesses of Old Europe*.

338. Girard, Philippe. *Haiti: The Tumultuous History—From Pearl of the Caribbean to Broken Nation*.

339. Girard, René. *Violence and the Sacred*.

340. Godwin, Joscelyn. *The Golden Thread: The Ageless Wisdom of the Western Mystery Traditions*.

341. Godwin, William. *Lives of the Necromancers: Or, an Account of the Most Eminent Persons in Successive Ages, Who Have Claimed for Themselves, or to Whom Has Been Imputed by Others, the Exercise of Magical Power*.

342. Gomez, Luis O. *Land of Bliss, the Paradise of the Buddha of Measureless Light: Sanskrit and Chinese Versions of the Sukha Vati Vyu Ha Sutras*.

343. Gooch, Stan. *Cities of Dreams: When Women Ruled the Earth*.

344. Gordon, Stuart. *The Encyclopedia of Myths and Legends*.

345. Gorer, Geoffrey. *Death, Grief, and Mourning*.

346. Gorer, Geoffrey. *The Life and Ideas of the Marquis de Sade*.

347. *Gospel of Thomas*.

348. Gosse, Philip Henry. *Omphalos*.

349. Gottschalk, Stephen. *The Emergence of Christian Science in American Religious Life*.

350. Gottschalk, Stephen. *Rolling Away the Stone: Mary Baker Eddy's Challenge to Materialism*.

351. Gracian, Baltasar. *The Art of Worldly Wisdom*.

352. Gracian, Baltasar. *The Critic*.

353. Grajetzki, Wolfram. *Burial Customs in Ancient Egypt: Life in Death for Rich and Poor*.

354. Graves, Robert. *The Greek Myths*.

355. Green, Miranda Aldhouse. *Dying for the Gods: Human Sacrifice in Iron Age and Roman Europe*.

356. Gruber, John. *EVP Lab 1.0.*

357. Gruman, Gerald. *A History of Ideas about the Prolongation of Life.*

358. Grundy, Stephan. *The Cult of Odinn: God of Death?*

359. Guiley, Rosemary. *The Guinness Encyclopedia of Ghosts and Spirits.*

360. Günther, Hans F. K. *The Religious Attitudes of the Indo-Europeans.*

361. Guthrie, William Keith. *Orpheus and Greek Religion.*

362. Guy, William Augustus. *Principles of Forensic Medicine.*

363. Gyatso, Geshe Kelsang. *Living Meaningfully, Dying Joyfully: The Profound Practice of Transference of Consciousness.*

364. Hadwen, Walter, William Tebb, and Edward Perry Vollum. *Premature Burial: How It May Be Prevented.*

365. Hall, Manly P. *The Secret Teachings of All Ages: An Encyclopedic Outline of Masonic, Hermetic, Qabbalistic and Rosicrucian Symbolical Philosophy.*

366. Hall, Manly P. *Twelve World Teachers: A Summary of Their Lives and Teachings.*

367. Halpern, Paul. *The Cyclical Serpent: Prospects for An Ever-Repeating Universe.*

368. Hammond, Paula. *Mini Monsters: Nature's Tiniest and Most Terrifying Creatures.*

369. Hanlon, Michael. *10 Questions Science Can't Answer (Yet): A Guide to the Scientific Wilderness.*

370. Hansen, William. *Phlegon of Tralles' Book of Marvels.*

371. Hanson, J. W. *The Bible Hell.*

372. Hanson, J. W. *Universalism, the Prevailing Doctrine of the Christian Church during its First Five Hundred Years.*

373. Harner, Michael. *The Way of the Shaman.*

374. Harrington, Alan. *The Immortalist: An Approach to the Engineering of Man's Divinity.*

375. Harris, Eleanor L. *Ancient Egyptian Divination and Magic.*

376. Harrison, Jane Ellen. *Prolegomena to the Study of Greek Religion.*

377. Hart, Hornell. *The Enigma of Survival.*

378. Hartshorne, Charles. *Omnipotence and Other Theological Mistakes.*

379. Harwood, William. *Mythology's Last Gods.*

380. Hasenfratz, Hans-Peter. *Barbarian Rites: The Spiritual World of the Vikings and the Germanic Tribes.*

381. Hassig, Ross. *Time, History, and Belief in Aztec and Colonial Mexico.*

382. Hassrick, Royal B. *The Sioux: Life and Customs of a Warrior Society.*

383. Hatab, Lawrence. *Nietzsche's Life Sentence: Coming to Terms with Eternal Recurrence.*

384. Henderson, Bruce. *Window to Eternity.*

385. Heretz, Leonid. *Russia on the Eve of Modernity: Popular Religion and Traditional Culture under the Last Tsars.*

386. Herlihy, Barbara. *The Human Body in Health and Illness.*

387. Herm, Gerhard. *The Celts: The People Who Came Out of the Darkness.*

388. *Hermetica: The Greek Corpus Hermeticum and the Latin Asclepius.*

389. Herodotus. *The Histories.*

390. Hesiod. *Theogony and Works and Days.*

391. Hick, John. *Death and Eternal Life.*

392. Hillman, James. *The Dream and the Underworld.*

393. Hinton, Charles Howard. *The Fourth Dimension.*

394. Hippolytus of Rome. *The Refutation of All Heresies.*

395. Hitti, Philip K. *Origins of the Druze People and Religion.*

396. Hogg, Gary. *Cannibalism and Human Sacrifice.*

397. Holmberg, Uno. *The Mythology of All Races. Finno-Ugric, Siberian.*

398. Holstein, Justus Frederick. *Rites and Ritual Acts as Prescribed by the Roman Religion According to the Commentary of Servius on Vergil's Aeneid.*

399. Howells, William. *The Heathens: Primitive Man and His Religions.*

400. Homer. *Iliad.*

401. Homer. *Odyssey.*

402. Hooke, S. H. *Labyrinth: Further Studies in the Relation between Myth and Ritual in the Ancient World.*

403. Hopkins, Keith, and Mary Beard. *The Colosseum.*

404. Hornung, Erik. *The Ancient Egyptian Books of the Afterlife.*

405. Hornung, Erik. *Conceptions of God in Ancient Egypt: The One and the Many.*

406. Hornung, Erik. *The Secret Lore of Egypt: Its Impact on the West.*

407. Hose, Charles. *The Pagan Tribes of Borneo: A Description of their Physical, Moral and Intellectual Condition, with some Discussion of their Ethnic Relations.*

408. Houellebecq, Michel. *H. P. Lovecraft: Against the World, Against Life.*

409. Howard, Michael. *Modern Wicca: A History from Gerald Gardner to the Present.*

410. Hoyle, Fred. *October the First Is Too Late.*

411. Hubbard, L. Ron. *Scientology: A History of Man.*

412. Hultgren, Arland J. *The Earliest Christian Heretics.*

413. Hultkrantz, Ake. *Native Religions of North America: The Power of Visions and Fertility.*

414. Hultkrantz, Ake. *The Religions of the American Indians.*

415. Hultkrantz, Ake. *Soul and Native Americans.*

416. Hume, David. *Dialogues Concerning Natural Religion.*

417. Hunt, Stoker, and Abigail Sturges. *Ouija: The Most Dangerous Game.*
418. Hutton, Ronald. *Pagan Britain.*
419. Hutton, Ronald. *The Triumph of the Moon: A History of Modern Pagan Witchcraft.*
420. Hyatt, Christopher S. *The Psychopath's Bible: For the Extreme Individual.*
421. Hynes, William J., and William G. Doty, eds. *Mythical Trickster Figures: Contours, Contexts, and Criticism.*
422. Iamblichus. *Theurgia; Or, The Egyptian Mysteries.*
423. Ikram, Salima. *Death and Burial in Ancient Egypt.*
424. Immortality Institute. *The Scientific Conquest of Death.*
425. Irenaeus. *Against Heresies.*
426. Isaak, Mark. *The Counter-Creationism Handbook.*
427. Iserson, Kenneth V. *Death to Dust: What Happens to Dead Bodies?*
428. Isya, Joseph. *Devil Worship; the Sacred Books and Traditions of the Yezidiz.*
429. Jacobson, Nils-Olof. *Life without Death?*
430. Jakobsson, Armann. "Vampires and Watchmen: Categorizing the Medieval Undead." *Journal of English and German Philology.*
431. Jaini, Jagmanderlal. *Outlines of Jainism.*
432. Jaini, P. S. *Jaina Path of Purification.*
433. James, E. O. *Origins of Sacrifice.*
434. James, E. O. *Prehistoric Religion: A Study in Prehistoric Archaeology.*
435. James, William. *Human Immortality.*
436. Janney, Rebecca Price. *Who Goes There? A Cultural History of Heaven and Hell.*
437. Jannot, Jean-René. *Religion in Ancient Etruria.*
438. Jastrow, Morris, Jr. *The Civilization of Babylonia and Assyria.*
439. Jaynes, Julian. *The Origin of Consciousness in the Breakdown of the Bicameral Mind.*
440. Jeans, James Hopwood. *The Mysterious Universe.*
441. Jefferson, Warren. *Reincarnation Beliefs of North American Indians: Soul Journey, Metamorphosis, and Near Death Experience.*
442. Johnsen, Linda. *The Complete Idiot's Guide to Hinduism.*
443. Johnston, Sarah Iles, ed. *Ancient Religions.*
444. Johnston, Sarah Iles. *Restless Dead: Encounters between the Living and the Dead in Ancient Greece.*
445. Johnstone, P. De Lacy. *Muhammad and his Power.*
446. Jones, Prudence, and Nigel Pennick. *A History of Pagan Europe.*
447. Jones, Richard H. *Science and Mysticism: A Comparative Study of Western Natural Science, Theravada Buddhism, and Advaita Vedanta.*
448. Joyce, James. *A Portrait of the Artist as a Young Man.*

449. Jung, Carl Gustav. *Man and His Symbols*.

450. Jung, Carl Gustav. *Memories, Dreams, Reflections*.

451. Jung, Carl Gustav. "Psychological Commentary on the Tibetan Book of the Dead."

452. Jung, Carl Gustav. *Synchronicity: An Acausal Connecting Principle*.

453. Jung, Carl Gustav. "Wotan."

454. Kaku, Michio. *Hyperspace: A Scientific Odyssey through Parallel Universes, Time Warps, and the 10th Dimension*.

455. Kaku, Michio. *Parallel Worlds: A Journey through Creation, Higher Dimensions, and the Future of the Cosmos*.

456. *Kalarnava Tantra*.

457. Kalweit, Holger. *Dreamtime and Inner Space: The World of the Shaman*.

458. Kamaluddin, Khwaja. *Four Lectures on Islam*.

459. Kapadia, Shapurji Aspaniarji. *The Teachings of Zoroaster, and the Philosophy of the Parsi Religion*.

460. Kaplan, Stephen. *Vampires Are*.

461. Karade, Baba Ifa. *The Handbook of Yoruba Religious Concepts*.

462. Kardec, Allan. *What is Spiritism?*

463. Kastenbaum, Robert, and Beatrice Kastenbaum. *Encyclopedia of Death: Myth, History, Philosophy, Science—The Many Aspects of Death and Dying*.

464. *Katha Upanishad*.

465. *Kaulavalinirnaya*.

466. Keen, Montague, Arthur Ellison, and David Fontana. *The Scole Report*.

467. Keith, Jim, ed. *Secret and Suppressed: Banned Ideas and Hidden History*.

468. Keith, Lierre. *The Vegetarian Myth: Food, Justice, and Sustainability*.

469. Kellaway, Jean. *The History of Torture and Execution: From Early Civilization through Medieval Times to the Present*.

470. Kellehear, Allan. *A Social History of Dying*.

471. Kemp, Barry. *How to Read the Egyptian Book of the Dead*.

472. Kerrigan, Michael. *The History of Death: Burial Customs and Funeral Rites, from the Ancient World to Modern Times*.

473. Kersten, Holger. *Jesus Lived in India: His Unknown Life Before and After the Crucifixion*.

474. Keulman, Kenneth. *Critical Moments in Religious History*.

475. Keuls, Eva C. *The Reign of the Phallus: Sexual Politics in Ancient Athens*.

476. Khaldun, Ibn. *The Muqaddimah: An Introduction to History*.

477. Khalil, Mohammad Hassan. *Between Heaven and Hell: Islam, Salvation, and the Fate of Others*.

478. Khazanov, Anatoly M. *Nomads and the Outside World*.

479. King, Francis. *Sexuality, Magic, and Perversion*.

480. Kingsland, Venika Mehra. *Hinduism—Simple Guides.*
481. Kinsley, David R. *Hindu Goddesses: Visions of the Divine Feminine in the Hindu Religious Tradition.*
482. Kirk, Robert. *The Secret Commonwealth of Elves, Fauns and Fairies.*
483. Kirkwood, Gordon MacDonald. *A Short Guide to Classical Mythology.*
484. Klimczuk, Stephen, and Gerald Warner. *Secret Places, Hidden Sanctuaries: Uncovering Mysterious Sights, Symbols, and Societies.*
485. Klossowski, Pierre. *Nietzsche and the Vicious Circle.*
486. Klostermaier, Klaus K. *Hinduism: A Short Introduction.*
487. Klostermaier, Klaus K. *A Survey of Hinduism.*
488. Knapp, Stephen. *Proof of Vedic Culture's Global Existence.*
489. Kohler, Kaufmann. *Heaven and Hell in Comparative Religion with Special Reference to Dante's Divine Comedy.*
490. *Koran.*
491. Kramer, Samuel Noah. *Sumerian Mythology.*
492. Kramer, Samuel Noah. *The Sumerians: Their History, Culture, and Character.*
493. Kripal, Jeffrey J. *Authors of the Impossible: The Paranormal and the Sacred.*
494. Kripal, Jeffrey J. *Mutants and Mystics: Science Fiction, Superhero Comics, and the Paranormal.*
495. Kuefler, Matthew. *The Manly Eunuch: Masculinity, Gender Ambiguity, and Christian Ideology in Late Antiquity.*
496. Kuper, Adam. *The Reinvention of Primitive Society: Transformations of a Myth.*
497. La Flesche, Francis. *Death and Funeral Customs among the Omahas.*
498. Lacarriere, Jacques. *The Gnostics.*
499. Lachman, Gary. *Madame Blavatsky: The Mother of Modern Spirituality.*
500. Lachman, Gary. *A Secret History of Consciousness.*
501. Lachman, Gary. *Swedenborg: An Introduction to His Life and Ideas.*
502. Lachman, Gary. *Turn Off Your Mind: The Mystic Sixties and the Dark Side of the Age of Aquarius.*
503. Laidlaw, James. *Riches and Renunciation: Religion, Economy, and Society among the Jains.*
504. Lamont-Brown, Raymond. *Kamikaze: Japan's Suicide Samurai.*
505. Lane, David. *Victory or Valhalla: The Final Compilation of Writings.*
506. Lane, Edward William. *Arab Society in the Time of the Thousand and One Nights.*
507. Lang, Andrew. *Magic and Religion.*
508. Lao Tzu. *Tao Te Ching.*
509. Laqueur, Walter. *No End to War: Terrorism in the Twenty-First Century.*

510. Larson, Jennifer. *Ancient Greek Cults: A Guide.*

511. Lauf, Detlef Ingo. *Secret Doctrines of the Tibetan Book of the Dead.*

512. Lavater, Lewes. *Of Ghosts and Spirits Walking by Night.*

513. *Laws of Manu.*

514. Lawson, E. Thomas. *Religions of Africa: Traditions in Transformation.*

515. *Laxdaela Saga.*

516. Lazenby, J. F. *The Spartan Army.*

517. Le Goff, Jacques. *The Birth of Purgatory.*

518. Lecouteux, Claude. *The Book of Grimoires: The Secret Grammar of Magic.*

519. Lecouteux, Claude. *The Return of the Dead: Ghosts, Ancestors, and the Transparent Veil of the Pagan Mind.*

520. Lecouteux, Claude. *The Secret History of Poltergeists and Haunted Houses: From Pagan Folklore to Modern Manifestations.*

521. Lecouteux, Claude. *The Tradition of Household Spirits: Ancestral Lore and Practices.*

522. Lecouteux, Claude. *Witches, Werewolves, and Fairies: Shapeshifters and Astral Doubles in the Middle Ages.*

523. Leon-Portilla, Miguel. *Aztec Thought and Culture: A Study of the Ancient Nahuatl Mind.*

524. Levi, Eliphas. *The History of Magic.*

525. Levi, Eliphas. *Transcendental Magic.*

526. Lewis, James R. *Encyclopedia of Death and the Afterlife.*

527. Lewis, James R., ed. *The Order of the Solar Temple: The Temple of Death.*

528. Lewis, Naphtali. *The Interpretation of Dreams and Portents in Antiquity.*

529. Lincoln, Bruce. *Death, War, and Sacrifice: Studies in Ideology and Practice.*

530. Lincoln, Bruce. *Myth, Cosmos, and Society: Indo-European Themes of Creation and Destruction.*

531. Lindow, John. *Norse Mythology: A Guide to Gods, Heroes, Rituals, and Beliefs.*

532. *Linga Purana.*

533. Lodru, Lama. *Bardo Teachings. The Way of Death and Rebirth.*

534. Long, Jeffrey D. *Jainism: An Introduction.*

535. Lopez, Donald S., Jr. *The Story of Buddhism: A Concise Guide to Its History and Teachings.*

536. Lopez, Donald S., Jr. *The Tibetan Book of the Dead: A Biography.*

537. Lovecraft, H. P. *The Complete Works of H. P. Lovecraft.* 2 vols.

538. Lowell, Percival. *Occult Japan; or, The Way of the Gods.*

539. Lucan. *Pharsalia.*

540. Luck, Georg. *Arcana Mundi: Magic and the Occult in the Greek and Roman Worlds: A Collection of Ancient Texts.*

541. MacCulloch, J. A. *The Mythology of All Races. Celtic and Slavic.*

542. MacCulloch, J. A. *The Mythology of All Races. Eddic Mythology.*

543. MacDougall, Duncan. "Hypothesis Concerning Soul-Substance, Together with Experimental Evidence of the Existence of Such Substance." *American Medicine.*

544. MacGregor, Geddes. *Images of Afterlife: Beliefs from Antiquity to Modern Times.*

545. MacGregor, Geddes. *Reincarnation in Christianity: A New Vision of the Role of Rebirth in Christian Thought.*

546. Mackenzie, Vicki. *Cave in the Snow.*

547. *Majjhima Nikaya.*

548. Mahabharata.

549. Malinowski, Bronislaw. *Sexual Life of Savages.*

550. Mallory, J. P. *In Search of the Indo-Europeans: Language, Archaeology and Myth.*

551. Malone, John. *Unsolved Mysteries of Science.*

552. Malpass, Michael A. *Daily Life in the Inca Empire.*

553. Manchester, Sean. *The Highgate Vampire: The Infernal World of the Undead Unearthed at London's Highgate Cemetery and Environs.*

554. Manchester, Sean. *Vampire Hunter's Handbook.*

555. Manniche, Lise. *Sexual Life in Ancient Egypt.*

556. Mantegazza, Paulo. *Sexual Relations of Mankind.*

557. *Manual of Indulgences (Roman Catholic).*

558. Mariner, William. *An Account of the Natives of the Tonga Islands, in the South Pacific Ocean.*

559. *Markandeya Purana.*

560. Martin, Raymond, and John Barresi. *The Rise and Fall of Soul and Self: An Intellectual History of Personal Identity.*

561. Masello, Robert. *Fallen Angels.*

562. Masello, Robert. *Raising Hell: A Concise History of the Black Arts and Those Who Dared to Practice Them.*

563. Masters, Anthony. *Devil's Dominion: The Complete Story of Hell and Satanism in the Modern World.*

564. *Matsya Purana.*

565. Matthews, Chris. *Modern Satanism: Anatomy of a Radical Subculture.*

566. Maxwell-Stuart, P. G. *Ghosts: A History of Phantoms, Ghouls, and Other Spirits of the Dead.*

567. May, Timothy. *The Mongol Art of War.*

568. McAllister, Peter. *Manthropology: The Science of Why the Modern Male Is Not the Man He Used to Be.*

569. McClelland, Norman C. *Encyclopedia of Reincarnation and Karma.*

570. McConkie, Bruce R. *Mormon Doctrine.*

571. McGhee, Robert. *The Last Imaginary Place: A Human History of the Arctic World.*

572. McGovern, William Montgomery. *Introduction to Mahayana Buddhism.*

573. McIntosh, Jane. *Handbook to Life in Prehistoric Europe.*

574. McKenna, Terence. *Food of the Gods: The Search for the Original Tree of Knowledge.*

575. McKeown, J. C. *A Cabinet of Greek Curiosities.*

576. McKeown, J. C. *A Cabinet of Roman Curiosities.*

577. McMahan, Ian. *Secrets of the Pharaohs.*

578. McTaggart, John Ellis. "The Unreality of Time." *Mind: A Quarterly Review of Psychology and Philosophy.*

579. Meagher, Robert E. *Herakles Gone Mad: Rethinking Heroism in an Age of Endless War.*

580. Meek, George W. *After We Die What Then?*

581. Meeks, Dimitri, and Christine Favard-Meeks. *Daily Life of the Egyptian Gods.*

582. Mencken, H. L. *The Philosophy of Friedrich Nietzsche.*

583. Mencken, H. L. *A Second Mencken Chrestomathy: A New Selection from the Writings of America's Legendary Editor, Critic, and Wit.*

584. Metraux, Alfred. *Voodoo in Haiti.*

585. Mew, James. *Traditional Aspects of Hell, Ancient and Modern.*

586. Meyer, Marvin W., ed. and trans. *The Gospel of Thomas: The Hidden Sayings of Jesus.*

587. Meyer, Marvin W., ed. *The Nag Hammadi Scriptures: The Revised and Updated Translation of Sacred Gnostic Texts Complete in One Volume.*

588. Milton, John. *Paradise Lost.*

589. Mirabello, Mark. *The Cannibal Within.*

590. Mirabello, Mark. *The Crimes of Jehovah.*

591. Mirabello, Mark. *Handbook for Rebels and Outlaws.*

592. Mirabello, Mark. *The Odin Brotherhood.*

593. Moncrieff, Malcolm M. *The Clairvoyant Theory of Perception.*

594. Monroe, Robert. *Far Journeys.*

595. Monroe, Robert. *Journeys Out of the Body.*

596. Monroe, Robert. *Ultimate Journey.*

597. Moody, Raymond. *Life After Life: The Investigation of a Phenomenon—Survival of Bodily Death.*

598. Moody, Raymond, and Paul Perry. *Reunions: Visionary Encounters with Departed Loved Ones.*

599. Morris, Ivan. *The Nobility of Failure: Tragic Heroes in the History of Japan.*

600. Mortensen, Karl. *A Handbook of Norse Mythology.*

601. Morton, W. Scott. *China: Its History and Culture.*

602. Moulton, James. *Early Zoroastrianism.*

603. Mueller, Friedrich Max. *Amitabha Sutra: The Smaller Sukhavati-Vyuha and the Infinite Sutra.*

604. Muir, William. *The Coran: Its Composition and Teaching.*

605. Muesse, Mark W. *The Hindu Traditions: A Concise Introduction.*

606. Muldoon, Sylvan. *The Case for Astral Projection: Hallucination or Reality!*

607. Muldoon, Sylvan. *Projection of the Astral Body.*

608. Muldoon, Sylvan. *Psychic Experiences of Famous People.*

609. Müller, Friedrich Max. *Natural Religion: The Gifford Lectures Delivered before the University of Glasgow.*

610. Murray, Margaret Alice. *The Splendor That Was Egypt: a General Survey of Egyptian Culture and Civilization.*

611. Myers, Frederic William Henry. *Human Personality and Its Survival of Bodily Death.*

612. Nabarz, Payam, and Caitlin Matthews. *The Mysteries of Mithras: The Pagan Belief That Shaped the Christian World.*

613. Nabokov, Vladimir. *Lolita.*

614. Nagarjuna. *Commentary on the Mahaprajnaparamita Sutra.*

615. Nahin, Paul J. *Time Travel: A Writer's Guide to the Real Science of Plausible Time Travel.*

616. Nakamura, Hajime. *A Comparative History of Ideas.*

617. Nansen, Fridtjof. *Eskimo Life.*

618. Nash, Jesse. "No More War Parties: The Pacification and Transformation of Plains Indian Religion" in *Critical Moments in Religious History* by Kenneth Keulman.

619. Nathan, John. *Mishima: A Biography.*

620. Nattier, Jan. *Once upon a Future Time: Studies in a Buddhist Prophecy of Decline.*

621. Neihardt, John G. *Black Elk Speaks: Being the Life Story of a Holy Man of the Oglala Sioux.*

622. Newquist, H. P., and Rich Maloof. *This Will Kill You: A Guide to the Ways in Which We Go.*

623. Nibley, Hugh W. *Teachings of the Pearl of Great Price.*

624. Nietzsche, Friedrich. *The Birth of Tragedy.*

625. Nietzsche, Friedrich. *Ecce Homo: How One Becomes What One Is.*

626. Nietzsche, Friedrich. *The Gay Science.*

627. Nietzsche, Friedrich. *Thus Spake Zarathustra.*

628. Nietzsche, Friedrich. *The Twilight of the Idols and The Anti-Christ: or How to Philosophize with a Hammer.*

629. Nietzsche, Friedrich. *The Will to Power.*

630. Nigosian, S. A. *The Zoroastrian Faith: Tradition and Modern Research.*

631. *Nilamata-Purana.*

632. Nilsson, Martin P. *A History of Greek Religion.*

633. Noory, George, and Rosemary Ellen Guiley. *Talking to the Dead.*

634. Norris, Robert. *Memoirs of the Reign of Bossa Ahadee, King of Dahomy, an Inland Country of Guiney.*

635. North, C. R. *An Outline of Islam.*

636. Novick, Rebecca. *Fundamentals of Tibetan Buddhism.*

637. Obayashi, Hiroshi, ed. *Death and Afterlife: Perspectives of World Religions.*

638. Obeyesekere, Gananath. *Imagining Karma: Ethical Transformation in Amerindian, Buddhist, and Greek Rebirth.*

639. O'Donoghue, Heather. *Old Norse-Icelandic Literature: A Short Introduction.*

640. Oesterreich, T. K. *Possession: Demoniacal and Other.*

641. O'Flaherty, Wendy Doniger. *Dreams, Illusion, and Other Realities.*

642. O'Flaherty, Wendy Doniger. *Karma and Rebirth in Classical Indian Traditions.*

643. O'Flaherty, Wendy Doniger. *The Origins of Evil in Hindu Mythology.*

644. O'Flaherty, Wendy Doniger. *Siva: The Erotic Ascetic.*

645. Ogden, Tom. *The Complete Idiot's Guide to Ghosts and Hauntings.*

646. Olberding, Amy, and Ivanhoe, Philip. *Mortality in Traditional Chinese Thought.*

647. Oldridge, Darren. *The Devil: A Very Short Introduction.*

648. Oldridge, Darren. *Strange Histories: The Trial of the Pig, the Walking Dead, and Other Matters of Fact from the Medieval and Renaissance Worlds.*

649. O'Neill, Richard. *Suicide Squads of World War II.*

650. Onians, R. B. *The Origins of European Thought: About the Body, the Mind, the Soul, the World, Time and Fate.*

651. Ono, Sokyo. *Shinto the Kami Way.*

652. Oosten, Jarich G. *The War of the Gods: The Social Code in Indo-European Mythology.*

653. Os, Van Bas. *Psychological Analyses and the Historical Jesus: New Ways to Explore Christian Origins.*

654. Osred. *Odinism: Present, Past and Future.*

655. Ouspensky, P. D. *The Fourth Way: An Arrangement by Subject of Verbatim Extracts from the Records of Ouspensky's Meetings in London and New York, 1921–46.*

656. Ouspensky, P. D. *A New Model of the Universe.*

657. Ouspensky, P. D. *Strange Life of Ivan Osokin.*

658. Ovid. *Metamorphoses.*

659. *Padma Purana.*

660. Padma Sambhava. *The Tibetan Book of the Dead: Awakening Upon Dying* (Version by Karma Lingpa, Elio Guarisco, Nancy Simmons, and Chogyal Namkhai Norbu).

661. Padma Sambhava. *The Tibetan Book of the Dead: First Complete Translation* (Version of Graham Coleman, Thupten Jinpa, Gyurme Dorje, and the Dalai Lama).

662. Padma Sambhava. *The Tibetan Book of the Dead: The Great Book of Natural Liberation Through Understanding in the Between* (Version by Robert Thurman, the Dalai Lama, and Karma Lingpa).

663. Padma Sambhava. *The Tibetan Book of the Great Liberation—Or The Method of Realizing Nirvana Through Knowing the Mind* (Version by W. Y. Evans-Wentz, C. G. Jung, Lama Kazi Dawa-Samdup, and Sir John Woodroffe).

664. Paine, Thomas. *The Age of Reason.*

665. Pallis, Marco. *Peaks and Lamas: A Classic Book on Mountaineering, Buddhism and Tibet.*

666. Palmer, Martin. *The Elements of Taoism.*

667. Palmer, Susan J. *Aliens Adored.*

668. Panati, Charles. *Extraordinary Endings of Practically Everything and Everybody.*

669. Panati, Charles. *Extraordinary Origins of Everyday Things.*

670. Panati, Charles. *Sacred Origins of Profound Things: The Stories Behind the Rites and Rituals of the World's Religions.*

671. Paper, Jordan D. *The Deities Are Many: A Polytheistic Theology.*

672. Parfrey, Adam. *Apocalypse Culture.*

673. Parfrey, Adam. *Apocalypse Culture II.*

674. Parfrey, Adam, and Kenn Thomas, eds. *Secret and Suppressed II: Banned Ideas and Hidden History into the 21st Century.*

675. Parmenides of Elea. *Fragments.*

676. Pascal, Blaise. *Pensees.*

677. Patch, Howard Rollin. *The Other World According to Descriptions in Medieval Literature.*

678. Pausanias. *Description of Greece.*

679. Peires, J. B. *The Dead Will Arise: Nongqawuse and the Great Xhosa Cattle-Killing Movement of 1856–7.*

680. Percy, William Armstrong, III. *Pederasty and Pedagogy in Archaic Greece.*

681. Petrie, W. M. Flinders. *The Religion of Ancient Egypt.*

682. Phipps, William E. *Muhammad and Jesus: A Comparison of the Prophets and Their Teachings.*

683. Pigott, Grenville. *A Manual of Scandinavian Mythology: Containing A Popular Account of the Two Eddas and of the Religion of Odin.*

684. Pike, David L. *Passage through Hell: Modernist Descents, Medieval Underworlds.*

685. Pinamonti, Giovanni Pietro. *Hell Opened to Christians.*

686. Pinch, Geraldine. *Magic in Ancient Egypt.*

687. Plato. *Critias.*

688. Plato. *Gorgias.*

689. Plato. *Laws.*

690. Plato. *Phaedrus.*

691. Plato. *Republic.*

692. Plato. *Symposium.*

693. Plato. *Timaeus.*

694. Plutarch. *Lives.*

695. Plutarch. *Morals.*

696. Poe, Edgar Allan. *Complete Tales and Poems.*

697. *Poetic Edda.*

698. Prabhavananda. *The Spiritual Heritage of India: A Clear Summary of Indian Philosophy and Religion.*

699. Price, H. H. "Survival and the Idea of 'Another World,'" *Proceedings of the Society of Psychical Research.*

700. Price, Neil. *Odin's Whisper: Death and the Vikings.*

701. Pringle, Heather. *The Mummy Congress: Science, Obsession, and the Everlasting Dead.*

702. Puckle, Bertram S. *Funeral Customs.*

703. Puhvel, Jaan. *Comparative Mythology.*

704. Quigley, Christine. *The Corpse: A History.*

705. Quinn, D. Michael. *Early Mormonism and the Magic World View.*

706. Rabinowitz, Jacob. *The Rotting Goddess: The Origin of the Witch in Classical Antiquity.*

707. Radin, Paul. *The Road of Life and Death.*

708. Radin, Paul. *The Winnebago Tribe.*

709. Rael. *Intelligent Design: Message from the Designers.*

710. Ramacharaka, Yogi. *The Life Beyond Death.*

711. Rancour-Laferriere, Daniel. *The Slave Soul of Russia: Moral Masochism and the Cult of Suffering.*

712. Randles, Jenny. *Breaking the Time Barrier: The Race to Build the First Time Machine.*

713. Randles, Jenny. *Time Travel: Fact, Fiction, and Possibility.*
714. Ranke-Heinemann, Uta. *Putting Away Childish Things.*
715. Rankin, Aidan. *The Jain Path: Ancient Wisdom for the West.*
716. Raphael, Simcha Paull. *Jewish Views of the Afterlife.*
717. Raudive, Konstantin. *Breakthrough.*
718. Read, Kay Almere. *Time and Sacrifice in the Aztec Cosmos.*
719. Reader, Ian. *Simple Guide to Shinto, the Religion of Japan.*
720. Redbeard, Ragnar. *Might Is Right.*
721. Rees, W. D. "The Hallucinations of Widowhood." *British Medical Journal.*
722. Reichel-Dolmatff, Gerardo. "Training for the Priesthood among the Kogi of Colombia." In Johannes Wilbert, ed. *Enculturation in Latin America: An Anthology.*
723. *Revelation of Rabbi Joshua ben Levi.*
724. Rice, Richard. *The Reign of God: An Introduction to Christian Theology from a Seventh-day Adventist Perspective.*
725. Richard, Carl J. *Why We're All Romans: The Roman Contribution to the Western World.*
726. Ridges, David J. *Doctrinal Details of the Plan of Salvation: From Premortality to Exaltation.*
727. Rielly, Robin L. *Kamikaze Attacks of World War II: A Complete History of Japanese Suicide Strikes on American Ships, by Aircraft and Other Means.*
728. *Rig Veda.*
729. Righi, Brian. *Ghosts, Apparitions and Poltergeists.*
730. Robertson, John Mackinnon. *Pagan Christs: Studies in Comparative Hierology.*
731. Rodman, Selden, and Carole Cleaver. *Spirits of the Night: The Vaudun Gods of Haiti.*
732. Rogo, D. Scott. *Haunted Universe.*
733. Rogo, D. Scott. *Life After Death: The Case for Survival of Bodily Death.*
734. Rogo, D. Scott. *Man Does Survive Death.*
735. Rogo, D. Scott. *Parapsychology: A Century of Inquiry.*
736. Rogo, D. Scott. *The Search for Yesterday.*
737. Rogo, D. Scott, and Raymond Bayless. *Phone Calls from the Dead.*
738. Rohde, Erwin. *Psyche: The Cult of Souls and Belief in Immortality among the Greeks.*
739. Romer, Frank E. *Pomponius Mela's Description of the World.*
740. Rose, H. J. *Primitive Culture In Italy.*
741. Rose, Jenny. *Zoroastrianism: An Introduction.*
742. Ross, Anne. *Pagan Celtic Britain.*

743. Ross, Catrien. *Supernatural and Mysterious Japan: Spirits, Hauntings and Paranormal Phenomena.*

744. Rucker, Rudolf. *The Fourth Dimension: A Guided Tour of the Higher Universes.*

745. Rucker, Rudolf B. *Geometry, Relativity and the Fourth Dimension.*

746. Rudwin, Maximilian Josef. *The Devil in Legend and Literature.*

747. Russell, Bertrand. *The Analysis of Mind.*

748. Russell, Jeffrey Burton. *The Devil: Perceptions of Evil from Antiquity to Primitive Christianity.*

749. Russell, Jeffrey Burton. *A History of Heaven.*

750. Russell, Jeffrey Burton. *Lucifer: The Devil in the Middle Ages.*

751. Russell, Jeffrey Burton. *Mephistopheles: The Devil in the Modern World.*

752. Russell, Jeffrey Burton. *The Prince of Darkness: Radical Evil and the Power of Good in History.*

753. Russell, Jeffrey Burton. *Satan: The Early Christian Tradition.*

754. Rustomji, Nerina. *The Garden and the Fire: Heaven and Hell in Islamic Culture.*

755. Sacks, Oliver. *Hallucinations.*

756. Safier, Joshua. *Yasukuni Shrine and the Constraints on the Discourses of Nationalism in Twentieth-Century Japan.*

757. *Saga of Faroemen.*

758. *Saga of Grettir the Strong.*

759. *Saga of King Hrolf Kraki.*

760. *Saga of the Volsungs.*

761. *Sagas of Ragnar Lodbrok (Saga of Ragnar Lodbrok, The Tale of Ragnar's Sons, and Ragnar's Death Song).*

762. Saggs, H. W. F. *Babylonians.*

763. Sallust. *On the Gods and the World.*

764. Sauneron, Serge. *The Priests of Ancient Egypt.*

765. Scheid, John. *An Introduction to Roman Religion.*

766. Schimmel, Annemarie. *Islam: An Introduction.*

767. Schmitt, Jean-Claude. *Ghosts in the Middle Ages: The Living and the Dead in Medieval Society.*

768. Schneider, Thomas. *Ancient Egypt in 101 Questions and Answers.*

769. Schofield, Alfred T. *Another World or the Fourth Dimension.*

770. Schopenhauer, Arthur. *The World as Will and Representation.*

771. Schreber, Daniel Paul. *Memoirs of My Nervous Illness.*

772. Schrodter, Willy. *Commentaries on the Occult Philosophy of Agrippa.*

773. Schrodter, Willy. *A Rosicrucian Notebook: The Secret Sciences Used by Members of the Order.*

774. Scot, Reginald. *The Discoverie of Witchcraft.*

775. Scott, George. *Phallic Worship: A History of Sex and Sexual Rites.*

776. Seler, Eduard. *Mexican and Central American Antiquities, Calendar Systems and History.*

777. Sen, Mala. *Death by Fire: Sati, Dowry Death, and Female Infanticide in Modern India.*

778. Shakespeare, William. *Hamlet.*

779. Shakespeare, William. *Richard II.*

780. Shakespeare, William. *Richard III.*

781. *Shatapatha Brahmana.*

782. Shea, Robert, and Robert Anton Wilson. *The Illuminatus! Trilogy: The Eye in the Pyramid, The Golden Apple, Leviathan.*

783. *Shi'ur Qomah.*

784. *Shiva Purana.*

785. Short, William R. *Icelanders in the Viking Age: The People of the Sagas.*

786. Shortland, Edward J. *Maori Religion and Mythology.*

787. Shushan, Gregory. *Conceptions of the Afterlife in Early Civilizations: Universalism, Constructivism and Near-Death Experience.*

788. Sibly, Ebenezer. *An Illustration of the Celestial Science of Astrology or The Art of Foretelling Future Events and Contingencies.*

789. Siculus, Diodorus. *Library of History.*

790. Simek, Rudolf. *Dictionary of Northern Mythology.*

791. Simon. *Papal Magic: Occult Practices within the Catholic Church.*

792. Simpkins, C. Alexander, and Annellen M. Simpkins. *Simple Buddhism: A Guide to Enlightened Living.*

793. Simpson, David. *A Discourse on Dreams and Night-visions, with Numerous Examples Ancient and Modern.*

794. Sjoestedt, Marie-Louise. *Celtic Gods and Heroes.*

795. *Skanda Purana.*

796. Slasher, Eddie. *Explorations Out of the Body: A Beginner's Roadmap to the Universe.*

797. Smith, Anthony. *The Mind.*

798. Smith, Christopher. *The Etruscans: A Very Short Introduction.*

799. Smith, Jane Idelman, and Yvonne Yazbeck Haddad. *The Islamic Understanding of Death and Resurrection.*

800. Smith, Joseph. *The Doctrine and Covenants.*

801. Smith, Joseph. *The Pearl of Great Price.*

802. Smith, Joseph Fielding. *Teachings of the Prophet Joseph Smith.*

803. Smith, Ken. *Ken's Guide to the Bible.*

804. Smith, Morton. *Jesus the Magician.*

805. Smith, William Robertson. *Religion of the Semites.*

806. Smith, William Robertson. "Sacrifice." *Encyclopedia Britannica.* Ninth edition, 1886.

807. Sorenson, Preben M. *The Unmanly Man: Concepts of Sexual Defamation in Early Northern Society.*

808. Soustelle, Jacques. *Daily Life of the Aztecs on the Eve of the Spanish Conquest.*

809. Spence, Lewis. *The Myths of Mexico and Peru.*

810. Spencer, A. J. *Death in Ancient Egypt.*

811. Spencer, Baldwin, and F. J. Gillen. *The Native Tribes of Central Australia.*

812. Spencer, Colin. *Vegetarianism: A History.*

813. Spencer, Robert. *The Politically Incorrect Guide to Islam.*

814. Spencer, Robert. *The Truth about Muhammad: Founder of the World's Most Intolerant Religion.*

815. Spickard, Paul, ed. *Race and Nation: Ethnic Systems in the Modern World.*

816. Spidle, Simeon. *The Belief in Immortality.*

817. St. Armand, Barton Levi. *H. P. Lovecraft: New England Decadent.*

818. Standage, Tom. *An Edible History of Humanity.*

819. Starhawk. *The Spiral Dance: A Rebirth of the Ancient Religion of the Goddess.*

820. Stein, R. A. *Tibetan Civilization.*

821. Steinhart, Eric. *On Nietzsche.*

822. Stevenson, Sinclair. *The Heart of Jainism.*

823. Stokes, Henry Scott. *The Life and Death of Yukio Mishima.*

824. Stone, Geo. *Suicide and Attempted Suicide: Methods and Consequences.*

825. Stone, Jon R., ed. *The Essential Max Müller: On Language, Mythology, and Religion.*

826. Storl, Wolf-Dieter. *Shiva: The Wild God of Power and Ecstasy.*

827. Stoyanov, Yuri. *The Other God: Dualist Religions from Antiquity to the Cathar Heresy.*

828. Strabo. *Geography.*

829. Streeter, Michael. *Behind Closed Doors.*

830. Sturluson, Snorri. *The Prose Edda.*

831. Sturluson, Snorri. *Ynglinga Saga.*

832. Summers, Montague. *The Vampire, His Kith and Kin.*

833. Summers, Montague. *The Vampire in Europe.*

834. Suzuki, Daisetz T. *Buddha of Infinite Light: The Teachings of Shin Buddhism, the Japanese Way of Wisdom and Compassion.*

835. Suzuki, Daisetz T. *An Introduction to Zen Buddhism.*

836. *Svarfæla Saga.*

837. Swain, Tony, and Garry Trompf. *The Religions of Oceania.*

838. Swann, Ingo. *Penetration—The Question of Extraterrestrial and Human Telepathy.*

839. Swanson, Guy E. *The Birth of the Gods: The Origin of Primitive Beliefs.*

840. Swedenborg, Emanuel. *Heaven and its Wonders and Hell: From Things Heard and Seen.*

841. Swedenborg, Emanuel, and Samuel M. Warren, ed. *A Compendium of the Theological and Spiritual Writings of Emanuel Swedenborg Being a Systematic and Orderly Epitome of All His Religious Works.*

842. Symonds, John. *The Magic of Aleister Crowley.*

843. Szasz, Thomas Stephen. *The Medicalization of Everyday Life: Selected Essays.*

844. Szasz, Thomas Stephen. *The Myth of Mental Illness: Foundations of a Theory of Personal Conduct.*

845. Szasz, Thomas Stephen. *Psychiatry: The Science of Lies.*

846. *Talmud (Genesis Rabbah).*

847. *Talmud (Pesikta Rabbati).*

848. *Talmud (Tractate Avodah Zarah).*

849. *Talmud (Tractate Gittin).*

850. *Talmud (Tractate Sanhedrin).*

851. Tardieu, Michael. *Manichaeism.*

852. Taube, Karl. *Aztec and Maya Myths.*

853. Taylor, John H. *Death and the Afterlife in Ancient Egypt.*

854. Teresi, Dick. *The Undead: Organ Harvesting, the Ice-Water Test, Beating Heart Cadavers—How Medicine Is Blurring the Line Between Life and Death.*

855. Tertullian. *On Monogamy.*

856. Tertullian. *A Treatise on The Soul.*

857. Thomas, Elizabeth Marshall. *The Harmless People.*

858. Thomas, Northcote Whitridge, *Crystal Gazing: Its History and Practice.*

859. Thomas, Spencer Lee Rogers. *The Shaman, His Symbols and His Healing Power.*

860. Thompson, John Eric Sidney. *A Commentary on the Dresden Codex: A Maya Hieroglyphic Book.*

861. Thompson, Ronald C. *God-Forsaken Trends in Sub-Saharan Africa.*

862. *Three Pure Land Sutras.*

863. Thurston, Herbert. *Ghosts and Poltergeists.*

864. Tibika, Françoise. *Molecular Consciousness: Why the Universe Is Aware of Our Presence.*

865. Tipler, Frank J. *The Physics of Immortality: Modern Cosmology, God and the Resurrection of the Dead.*

866. Tompkins, Peter, and Christopher Bird. *The Secret Life of Plants.*

867. Trompf, G. W. *Melanesian Religion.*

868. Trudeau, Richard. *Universalism 101: An Introduction for Leaders of Unitarian Universalist Congregations.*

869. Tucker, Elizabeth. *Haunted Halls: Ghostlore of American College Campuses.*

870. Tulpe, Irvina, and Eugeny A Torchinov. "The Castrati ("Skoptsy") Sect in Russia: History, Teaching, and Religious Practice." *The International Journal of Transpersonl Studies.*

871. Turcan, Robert. *The Cults of the Roman Empire.*

872. Turcan, Robert. *The Gods of Ancient Rome: Religion in Everyday Life from Archaic to Imperial Times.*

873. Turlington, Shannon R. *The Complete Idiot's Guide to Voodoo.*

874. Turnbull, Colin. *The Forest People.*

875. Turner, Alice K. *The History of Hell.*

876. Turville-Petre, Gabriel. *Myth and Religion of the North: The Religion of Ancient Scandinavia.*

877. Tylor, Edward Burnett. *Primitive Culture: Researches into the Development of Mythology, Philosophy, Religion, Language, Art and Custom.*

878. Tyrell, George N.M. *Apparitions.*

879. Tyson, Donald. *The Dream World of H. P. Lovecraft: His Life, His Demons, His Universe.*

880. Uman, Martin A. *All about Lightning.*

881. Underhill, Ruth Murray. *Red Man's Religion: Beliefs and Practices of the Indians North of Mexico.*

882. Unno, Taitetsu. *River of Fire, River of Water.*

883. Upanishads.

884. Urban, Hugh B. *The Church of Scientology: A History of a New Religion.*

885. Ustinova, Yulia. *Caves and the Ancient Greek Mind: Descending Underground in the Search for Ultimate Truth.*

886. Valiente, Doreen. *An ABC of Witchcraft Past and Present.*

887. Vallee, Jacques. *Dimensions: A Casebook of Alien Contact.*

888. Vallee, Jacques. *Messengers of Deception: UFO Contacts and Cults.*

889. Van Eeden, Frederik. "A Study of Dreams." *Proceedings of the Society for Psychical Research.*

890. Venkatesananda, Swami. *The Concise Yoga Vasistha.*

891. Vernant, Jean-Pierre. *Mortals and Immortals.*

892. Vernant, Jean-Pierre. *Myth and Society in Ancient Greece.*

893. Vernant, Jean-Pierre. *The Origins of Greek Thought.*

894. Veyne, Paul. *Did the Greeks Believe in Their Myths?: An Essay on the Constitutive Imagination.*

895. *Vinland Sagas* (*Saga of Eric the Red* and *Saga of the Greenlanders*).

896. Virgil. *Aeneid.*

897. Virgil. *Georgics.*

898. *Vishnu Purana.*

899. Vonnegut, Kurt. *Slaughterhouse-Five.*

900. Vulliamy, C. E. *Immortality: Funerary Rites and Customs.*

901. Waddell, L. A. *Tibetan Buddhism.*

902. Waite, A. E. *The Book of Ceremonial Magic: Including the Rites and Mysteries of Goetic Theurgy, Sorcery, and Infernal Necromancy.*

903. Waite, A. E. *The Holy Grail: History, Legend and Symbolism.*

904. Walker, James R. *Lakota Belief and Ritual.*

905. Walker, James R. "Sun Dance and Other Ceremonies of the Oglala Division of the Teton Dakota." In *Anthropological Papers of the American Museum of Natural History.*

906. Wall, O. A. *Sex and Sex Worship.*

907. Wallace, Alfred Russel. *Miracles and Modern Spiritualism.*

908. Wallace, Earnest, and E. Adamson Hoebel. *The Comanches: Lords of the South Plains.*

909. Warraq, Ibn. *Why I Am Not a Muslim.*

910. Warren, Herbert. *Jainism in Western Garb as a Solution to Life's Great Problems.*

911. Warrior, Valerie M. *Roman Religion.*

912. Waterhouse, John W. *Zoroastrianism.*

913. Waters, Frank. *Book of the Hopi.*

914. Watson, Lyall. *Beyond Supernature: A New Natural History of the Supernatural.*

915. Watson, Lyall. *The Nature of Things: The Secret Life of Inanimate Objects.*

916. Webster, Kenneth. *The Vertical Plane.*

917. Weinberger-Thomas, Catherine. *Ashes of Immortality: Widow-Burning in India.*

918. Welch, Holmes. *The Practice of Chinese Buddhism, 1900–1950.*

919. Wesson, Robert. "Is Your Brain Really Necessary?" *Science.*

920. White, Andrew Dickson. *History of the Warfare of Science with Theology in Christendom.* 2 vols.

921. White, Anna, and Leila S. Taylor. *Shakerism: Its Meaning and Message.*

922. White, Jon Manchip. *Everyday Life of the North American Indian.*

923. White, Matthew. *Atrocities: The 100 Deadliest Episodes in Human History.*

924. Wickland, Carl. *Thirty Years among the Dead.*

925. Wiedemann, Alfred. *The Ancient Egyptian Doctrine of the Immortality of the Soul.*

926. Wiedemann, Alfred. *The Realms of the Egyptian Dead: According to the Belief of the Ancient Egyptian.*

927. Wiedemann, Alfred. *Religion of the Ancient Egyptians.*

928. Wilcock, David. *The Hidden Science of Lost Civilisations: The Source Field Investigations.*

929. Wilde, Oscar. *The Picture of Dorian Gray.*

930. Wiley, Kristi L. *The A to Z of Jainism.*

931. Wilkins, Robert. *Death: A History of Man's Obsessions and Fears.*

932. Wilkins, W. J. *Hindu Mythology, Vedic and Puranic.*

933. Wilkinson, J. Gardner. *The Ancient Egyptians.*

934. Williams, Drew. *The Complete Idiot's Guide to Understanding Mormonism.*

935. Williams, Thomas. *Fiji and the Fijians.*

936. Wilson, Colin. *Poltergeist: A Classic Study in Destructive Hauntings.*

937. Wilson, Colin. *The Strange Life of P. D. Ouspensky.*

938. Wilson, Ian. *Jesus: The Evidence.*

939. Wilson, Robert Anton. *Cosmic Trigger I.*

940. Wilson, Robert Anton. *Cosmic Trigger II.*

941. Wilson, Robert Anton. *Cosmic Trigger III.*

942. Wilson, Robert Anton. *Everything Is Under Control: Conspiracies, Cults, and Cover-ups.*

943. Wilson, Robert Anton. *The New Inquisition.*

944. Winslow, Jacques-Bénigne. *The Uncertainty of the Signs of Death, and the Danger of Precipitate Internments and Dissections, Demonstrated.*

945. Withnell, John G. *The Customs and Traditions of the Aboriginal Natives of North Western Australia.*

946. Wolf, Jack. *The Way of the Odin Brotherhood.*

947. Wood, Charles L. *The Mormon Conspiracy.*

948. Wood, Randall, and Carmine DeLuca. *Dictator's Handbook: A Practical Manual for the Aspiring Tyrant.*

949. Woodroffe, John. "Preface to the Tibetan Book of the Dead."

950. Woolley, Charles Leonard. *The Sumerians.*

951. *Yajur Veda.*

952. Yarrow, H. C. *Introduction to the Study of Mortuary Customs among the North American Indians.*

953. Yates, Frances. *The Occult Philosophy in the Elizabethan Age.*

954. *Yoga Vasistha.*

955. Yoganada, Paramhansa. *Karma and Reincarnation.*

956. Zaehner, R. C. *The Dawn and Twilight of Zoroastrianism.*

957. Zaehner, R. C. *Teachings of the Magi: Compendium of Zoroastrian Beliefs.*

958. Zaleski, Carol. *Otherworld Journeys: Accounts of Near-Death Experience in Medieval and Modern Times.*

959. Zaloga, Steven. *Kamikaze: Japanese Special Attack Weapons 1944–45.*

960. Zarandi, Merhdad M., and Giovanni Monastra. *Science and the Myth of Progress.*

961. Zeitlin, Froma I., and John J. Winkler. *Before Sexuality.*

962. Zimmer, Heinrich Robert. *Myths and Symbols in Indian Art and Civilization.*

963. Zimmer, Heinrich Robert, and Joseph Campbell. *Philosophies of India.*

964. Zimmerman, John Edward. *The Dictionary of Classical Mythology.*

965. *Zohar* (Kabbalah).

Index